REFLECTIONS

Bright Days Do Come is an awe-inspiring read that gives example after example of signs from our loved ones, which adds to the growing evidence that we don't die. It is an insightful book that pulls you into Karin's journey and leaves you with inspiration on how to get signs and messages from your loved ones.

— SANDRA CHAMPLAIN, AUTHOR OF THE #1
INTERNATIONAL BESTSELLER, *WE DON'T DIE – A SKEPTIC'S DISCOVERY OF LIFE AFTER DEATH* AND
HOST OF THE PODCASTS *WE DON'T DIE RADIO* AND
SHADES OF THE AFTERLIFE

In Bright Days Do Come, Karin invites us into the space where grief and love coexist. After losing her brother, Brian, Karin shows us that love does not disappear when a life ends — it changes form. She shares not only her grief, but the ways Brian's love has continued to reach her through signs and moments of connection. Her writing is brave, compassionate, and deeply vulnerable. This memoir is a tender offering to anyone learning how to carry loss while still opening their heart to life.

— HEATHER VANDERMEYDEN, AUTHOR OF
MIRACLES FROM THE OTHER SIDE

What a gorgeous book Karin has written. Bright Days Do Come is detailed and vulnerable and you will find yourself looking at all of life differently after reading her words. I was profoundly inspired by her attitude toward life, both here and beyond, and am inspired to show up each day expecting more love, connection, and beauty. Yes, there is tragedy and grief woven throughout the book, but they're dwarfed by what she and other players in the stories have learned about resilience, joy, living with your whole heart, and family.

— EMILY BURNETT, AUTHOR OF *DEAR FELLOW SPENDER* AND *DEAR FELLOW DREAMER*

BRIGHT DAYS DO COME

A JOURNEY OF LOSS, LIGHT, AND SIGNS FROM BEYOND

KARIN MCLEAN

Bozich Towne Publishing

To my children, Ever and Sola:

I leave behind these words as a legacy for you and generations to come. Please take them to heart and know that once I've left this Earth, I will still be right here with you and will do everything I can to send you signs. I ask that you do everything you can to be open to receiving them. I am eternally grateful to have been given the best gift I could have ever been given—being your mother. I love you up to the stars and back, forever and always!

Love, Mom

CONTENTS

DEAR READER

For the first 18 years of my life, I was religious but not spiritual—
and now I am the opposite: spiritual, but not religious. I lost my
little brother at that age, and losing him, along with the challenges
I've faced, has changed me. Until my brother passed, I never knew
that our departed loved ones could send us signs from the other
side. The signs I've received have shown me that our consciousness
continues after we leave our bodies behind. My hope is that the
words I share in this book will bring you comfort in knowing that
receiving signs from loved ones is possible.

Death is going to happen to all of us, whether we want it to or
not—but it is not the end. According to the law of conservation of
energy, energy can neither be *created* nor *destroyed*; it can only be
transformed from one form to another. Because of this, it is reasonable to believe that the energy we are made of doesn't just go away
when we shed our physical bodies; it only changes form. That
makes it equally reasonable to believe that our energy doesn't just
begin when we are born here on Earth. I believe that we existed
before we came here, and that we will continue to exist after we

leave, just like the infinity symbol—there is no beginning, and there is no end.

In this book, I take you on my journey of loss, light, and signs from beyond. I am here to share what I have come to understand as my truths, and I encourage you to take what resonates with you and leave the rest. That is what I like about spirituality: as you go along your path in life, you can adopt what makes sense to you and let go of what doesn't—it's an ever-evolving process. I try not to hold too tightly to the beliefs that I have picked up along my way, as I know that they will transform as I continue on this adventure called life. But, because of the things I've experienced and share here, my belief in the afterlife is one that I will always carry.

Before we begin, let me start by telling you about one of my favorite publications: "Deep Thoughts," written by humorist and author Jack Handey. "Deep Thoughts" debuted in 1991 on *Saturday Night Live* (SNL) and played as segments between sketches until 1998. Handey describes them as "irreverent observations on life," which I feel represents them perfectly.

In the pages that follow, you will come to find that 1991 was a significant year for me and my family. "Deep Thoughts" brought us a lot of much-needed laughter during that time, acting like a ray of sunshine, and I looked forward to watching SNL every week because of them.

While the topic of my book is quite the opposite of irreverent, I must open with a little bit of humor, as humor helps open the heart and raise our vibration. So, I'm honored to share one of my most favorite "Deep Thoughts:"

"Whenever you read a good book, it's like the author is right there, in the room, talking to you, which is why I don't like to read good books."

I hope this made you laugh and helped open your heart, so that as you read my book, you will feel like I *truly* am right there, in the room, talking to you. I'd like you to imagine that we are sitting next to each other on a cozy couch as I share my journey, my truths, and these goosebump-inducing signs with you.

And just maybe, you'll find it the reason that you like to read good books.

I have felt deeply inspired to share these experiences that I, and others, have had, so that they are not forgotten. If we don't document our stories, they follow us to the grave. Yes, we will carry our experiences with us into the afterlife, but if we write them down, they can live on for those temporarily left behind.

The following quote, by novelist Isaac Bashevis Singer, portrays how important it is to write down our experiences. This message—paired with what felt like persistent nudging from Spirit, eventually inspired me to write this book.

"When a day passes,
It is no longer there.

What remains of it?
Nothing more than a story.

If stories weren't told or
Books weren't written,
Man would live like beasts—
Only for the day.

Today we live, but tomorrow,
Today will be a story.

The whole world, all human life,
Is one long story."

And so, my story begins…

PART I

MY JOURNEY

I wrote this poem as I sat in my bed at the rehabilitation center, just one month after my entire world was turned upside down. With pen and journal in hand, thoughts swirled through my mind about how unpredictable life can be, and how everything can change in the blink of an eye.

EMOTIONAL WEATHER

Life is like the weather,
It changes from day to day.
Like the rain,
Many tears fall.
Like the wind,
Things blow in and out of life.
Like a storm,
You don't know what to expect.
Like the sun,
Bright days do come.

—Karin Bozich, November 1991

As I write this book now, 33 years later, with my fingertips at the keyboard, thoughts swirl through my mind about all that has happened and how I can now see the gifts that arose from the trials.

Life can be very hard at times, and it can be very good at times, but the key phrase is "at times." Life is not static; things are always changing—just like the weather. When we experience life's storms, we appreciate the bright days that much more. I have found that with every storm we go through, there is always something positive that can be found, even if it is simply a lesson learned. You may not see the positives right away, but in hindsight, I have found that "bright days *do* come."

THE ACCIDENT

On October 4, 1991, my life and my family's lives were changed forever. All of us, except for my dad, were involved in a single-car rollover while traveling on the freeway. From my viewpoint, one minute I'm entering a new phase of life as a college student, and the next minute, those plans are put on hold and I hear my dad's voice telling me, "Karin, you were in a very bad car accident." I thought to myself, "What is going on? Am I dreaming?" I felt exhausted, and all I could see was a sliver of the world around me, which made what I was trying to absorb feel more like fiction than reality. I questioned why my surroundings looked so dim, and was met with the answer that my eyes were significantly swollen and bruised, caused by fracturing the base of my skull.

My dad continued, "You were ejected from the car, and both of your femurs were broken." I was utterly shocked to hear this uncanny news, as I had often thought to myself that one of the worst things that could ever happen to a person would be to break both legs at the *same* time. I was in disbelief that this was now my truth. I was told that my legs now housed two titanium rods, which ran the length of my thighs, and there were more surgeries to come over the span of the next several days.

The force of my body hitting the ground caused severe bruising of my chest wall, a broken left clavicle bone, and the collapse of both lungs. As I floated in and out of consciousness, my nutrients were delivered through plastic tubes, while a ventilator had taken over the breaths that were once my own. A mixture of medications and the blood of generous strangers flowed through my veins, as my sleeping and waking moments became entangled, leaving only blurred memories behind.

As each day passed, my waking moments began to outweigh my sleeping moments, and I came to learn of the rest of my injuries —most of which were on my left side, where I had landed. My left knee was fractured, and my forehead was adorned with a large gauze bandage, covering my newly acquired abrasions and lacerations.

I had also sustained multiple facial fractures: my left orbital floor had been shattered, the upper part of my left jaw was fractured, and my cheekbone had a fracture which herniated into the bones around the left side of my nose. Additionally, my nose was broken, which displaced my septum to the left. Once I became more coherent, I was told that a plate and screws had been surgically placed under my left eye, acting as my new orbital floor to prop the tissues back into place. The surgeons repaired my nose to the best of their ability, but due to the nasal tracheal tube that needed to stay in place, the repair was limited.

Obviously, the surgeries were necessary and lifesaving, and I am beyond grateful for them. But, learning about my surgeries, *after* the fact, felt like there had been an invasion of my body. My limited vision and medicated daze intensified the bizarre feeling of this horrific nightmare. If only I could just wake up!

At the time of the accident, my family and I had been traveling southbound on the freeway in our brand-new Subaru Legacy station wagon. We left around three o'clock in the afternoon on a sunny, yet slightly crisp, day in early October. In the car were my mom, my three siblings, and me—totaling five of us. My mom, Irene, 46, sat in the front passenger seat, while my sister Erika, 16, drove. The back seats held my sister Kristin, 14, behind my mom, and me, 18, behind Erika. The youngest, Brian, nine years old, curled up in the very back seat. My parents had divorced many years earlier, and for this reason, my dad was not traveling with us.

1987: Erika, 12 (bottom left); Kristin, 10 (middle left); Karin, 14 (top); Irene, 42 (right); and Brian, 5 (center)

Erika held a brand-new driver's license, so she took to the wheel to gain more driving experience, while sips of cola kept her alert. At almost an hour into the drive, she leaned in for a sip and took her eyes off the wheel for a split second—one split second that changed everything. As she looked up, she was surprised to see that we were drifting to the right. She panicked as she turned the steering wheel to correct herself, but the adrenaline rush caused her to pull harder than she had intended to. Consequently, control over the car was lost as we overcorrected and rolled four times, crossing the median. Luckily, there were no other vehicles involved.

Those of us in the back seats were not wearing seat belts, and as a result, we were ejected as the car rolled. Although we had been heading south, once our car finally stopped rolling, it was facing north, on the northbound side of the freeway. It's astonishing that our car rolled all the way to the opposite side of the freeway—and changed direction. Fortunately, the car came to rest right-side up, but the tires were all blown out. The roof, and sides of the car, were now crushed—holding Erika and my mom hostage in the front seats. Eventually, the Jaws of Life were used to peel back the roof of the car to set them free.

Droves of people stopped to help, including many health professionals. My mom eventually received a list of the volunteers, which held the names of thirty people, in addition to the ambulance crew. The state trooper at the scene, Randy Ingram, stated, "In an age where people are accused of refusing to get involved, it was nothing short of amazing." Of the thirty volunteers, 10 of them were Registered Nurses, and one of them was an Emergency Room doctor! Ingram continued, "So many people stopped to help the victims. I've never seen anything like it."

The Emergency Room doctor, Brent Mabey, happened to be traveling directly behind our car, along with his wife Mary who was an RN, and their six children. Caravanning behind them were two more cars, filled with their friends and their families. They were traveling from Salt Lake City, Utah, to Anaheim, California, to visit Disneyland. As they drove behind us, both Dr. Mabey and his wife wondered what was going on with our car, as it was starting to slightly weave. Shortly after the car began to weave, it overcorrected and began rolling.

Once our car came to a stop, Dr. Mabey, whose specialty is trauma medicine, pulled over, grabbed the medical kit that he had in his car, and he and Mary immediately ran to our aid. One of the other parents, who had been caravanning behind them, pulled over and stayed with the Mabeys' children to shield them from witnessing the tragic scene. As Dr. Mabey approached me, his initial prognosis was that *if* I lived, I'd lose both legs. Luckily, he saved my life *and* my legs!

A semi-truck driver stopped his truck on a diagonal, to help divert traffic away from the scene. In Dr. Mabey's medical kit, he had one bottle of saline solution, which he poured directly into the open cavity of my right femur, which was broken and protruding through the skin. The saline solution played a significant role in warding off infection in that leg. I was losing so much blood because of the open wound, that I ended up needing a blood transfusion at some point.

In addition to the compound fracture in my right leg, Dr. Mabey was also very concerned about my left leg, because not only was it broken, but my hip was badly twisted and dislocated, putting pressure on the vessels, therefore cutting off blood supply. With the help of volunteers, Dr. Mabey was able to thrust my left hip back into place, allowing the flow of blood to return to my leg. He was also worried that some of my ribs were fractured; luckily, none were, except one back rib that was slightly pushed out of place, which still is to this day.

My family and I believe it was divine intervention that an ER doctor happened to be driving behind us to help at the scene of our accident. One of the parents who had been caravanning behind the Mabeys' car, named Martha, offered comfort and reassurance to my mom and Erika, while they waited for the Jaws of Life to arrive. My mom remembers being able to hear *some* of us, but not *all* of us, and I'm sure the wait seemed like an eternity. Not having the ability to rush to our side, while also trying to decipher who was crying out and who wasn't, has got to be the most unthinkable agony for a mother to have to suffer through.

Martha remembers holding my mom's hand and keeping a tight lip from saying anything that might alarm her. She stated, "I think of your family often, and wish we could have done more. You are quite the family." She continued, "It was traumatic for everybody. There was so much running around, that even the patrol man was unsure of what to do. It was obvious that Dr. Mabey was in charge. There were so many wonderful people who stopped and asked what they could do to help." She also mentioned how that day will be forever etched into the memories of everyone who stopped at the scene. When she said that to me, I took pause, as I'd never thought about how witnessing a trauma like that could have impacted the volunteers—it was quite the realization.

Months after the accident, my family and I met with Dr. Mabey and Mary, because we had so many unanswered questions. Additionally, as I wrote this book, I called the Mabeys to clarify some things that were still unclear to me after all these years. It was so helpful to get my questions answered. It had been a mystery to my family how Kristin, Brian, and I managed to get thrown from the car without getting crushed by it. Mary recalls, "It looked like people were getting shot out of a cannon, like in a circus." When I heard this, I shuddered from deep within as the imagery found itself a place in my memory bank. She remembered seeing someone in a green T-shirt, and two people in red shirts, *flying* out of the car —I was wearing the green shirt that day.

It had always been a mystery to us as to where we landed. The Mabeys shared that Kristin and I landed in the dirt of the median, which made sense as to why there was so much dirt in the open wound of my right leg. They said that Brian landed on the asphalt of the northbound side of the freeway, which was extremely difficult to hear. Dr. Mabey recalls quickly going around to all of us to confirm we were coherent, stating, "It was important to ensure that you were all 'with it' enough to know your names." He said that we were all conscious, except for Brian, and that Kristin and I were "delirious and uncertain of our surroundings." But even so, she and I were able to respond with our names.

He also shared, "At the scene of an accident, you address the problems that you can, in the little bit of time that you have." Mary said that because Dr. Mabey had his medical kit with him, he was able to get some interventions going, like antibiotics and IVs, before the paramedics even arrived. He happened to have one dose of a narcotic in his kit, and he administered that to me.

Mary recalled, "It was interesting to see my husband in action, because I never get to see him on-the-job. He went right into 'doctor mode,' barking orders to volunteers, and assigning them to victims; the next day, his voice was so hoarse." Dr. Mabey assigned a volunteer to hold my head and keep it from moving, while he went to check on everyone else. Kristin was arching her back, so he assigned volunteers to hold her still, as it was important that she didn't move her spine, in case of a spinal cord injury. There were so many kind souls who gave us their time and support. My family and I are forever grateful for the help we received.

Our accident happened eight miles south of the small town of Nephi, Utah, and Kristin, Brian, and I were initially taken by ambulance to the closest hospital: Central Valley Medical Center, in Nephi. Dr. Mabey accompanied us there; however, the medical center wasn't equipped to handle trauma patients, so upon our arrival, three helicopters awaited to deliver us to hospitals in Salt Lake City, 84 miles north. First, Brian was sent to Primary Children's Hospital, and second, Kristin was sent to LDS Hospital. I was the last to go, because both the ER doctor *and* the life-flight team were having issues inserting the breathing tube into me. After many attempts, they asked Dr. Mabey to try, and he was successful. Once I was intubated, I was loaded into the helicopter to be taken to LDS Hospital, where Kristin was already headed. I am grateful for Dr. Mabey's recollection, as I still don't recall these events.

As Dr. Mabey watched me take flight, he could finally take a big, deep breath. In that moment, it dawned on him that everything looked darker than it should, and he realized that he'd been wearing his sunglasses the *entire* time! He had been so laser-focused on assisting us, that he truly had been immersed in doctor mode. With everything he did at the scene for all of us, and with being able to intubate me when all other attempts had failed, he was instrumental in saving my life, and is truly my hero.

The accident resulted in many injuries for all of us—both emotional and physical. I am heartbroken to say that the accident resulted in Brian losing his life, and Kristin and I coming *extremely* close to losing ours. We all could have been killed that day, and we are very lucky to be here. We miss Brian more than we can express, but as you will read in the pages that follow, he is still with us.

Of the numerous people who stopped to help, one very special individual was Mary Lou Klippel, who was an RN at the time. On the day of our accident, she was traveling with her children, running late, and should have been at their intended destination one hour earlier. She could see that there was a serious accident ahead, so she pulled over to help, but kept her children in the car. At the scene, she ran from victim to victim, working with the paramedics to help stabilize us, start IV's, and offer comfort. She remembers being at Brian's side and "feeling his spirit leave." Although I don't doubt that she "felt his spirit leave," I believe Brian left his body before he experienced any pain. I imagine his spirit lingered briefly before leaving the scene—perhaps that's what she felt. She testified to her family that she felt like she was destined to be there, at that time, on that day.

2

THE HOSPITAL

Upon my arrival, the medical team discovered that a medium-sized pebble was sitting on my windpipe, which was significantly adding to my breathing issues. A thin, flexible tube was inserted into the airways, and they used specialized tools to remove it. In addition to this, my heartbeat was so faint that a pulse could barely be detected.

Initially, I stayed in the Shock Trauma Unit. From there, I was taken to the Intensive Care Unit. And lastly, I was moved to a regular room—but most of that remains a blur. My Uncle Orin stayed beside me during one of my first nights in the hospital, but I don't remember that. There are only a handful of memories that I have from my time in the hospital, which I credit to the trauma I experienced, the heavy sedation I was under, and the surgeries that transpired. I also partially assign my lack of memories throughout this period to the limited vision I had because of my swollen eyes, as vision and memory go hand in hand.

One of the first memories I have was seeing a schoolmate whom I had known since kindergarten, hovering over me. Seeing her face above mine was utterly confusing—especially with not being able to see very well. It turns out that this acquaintance, Traci, who is now a good friend of mine, worked as a phlebotomist at the hospital. She was checking my blood after my transfusion, and I remember asking, "Traci?!" like it was the biggest question of my life, as I drifted back to sleep.

Another memory was of a woman who came into my room to assess my mental condition by asking me some questions. Although I couldn't see well, I observed that she held a clipboard for noting my responses. She asked if I could state my name, the year, and who the current president was. I replied with my full name, the year (1991), and Bugs Bunny as president. She gasped after I told her that Bugs Bunny was president, but let out a sigh of relief as I informed her that the current president was George Bush, and I was just kidding. I knew that she was trying to confirm whether my intellect was still intact, so I had to tease her—just a little bit.

Once I was moved out of the ICU, nurses would come into my room to help me transfer from my hospital bed to a chair, as sitting up versus lying down helps prevent blood clots from developing. One day, after moving to the chair, I came face-to-face with my thigh, and saw the scar where my bone had originally broken through. I found it hard to believe that it was mine—it was the size of my palm, and shaped like the letter Y. There were stitches poking out through my skin, as if to eerily introduce themselves, while resembling a sewing project gone wrong.

The most poignant memory I have from the hospital was when my mom and my Aunt Sheila entered my room while I was sleeping. As the door shut behind them, it startled me from my slumber. I then overheard my Aunt Sheila asking my mom, "Does she know about Brian yet?" I went from being asleep to fully alert in 0.1 seconds, as my heart began to pound out of my chest and my head filled with worry. While I was still unable to see much, I mentally braced myself as I frantically yelled out, "What are you talking about? What happened to Brian?" My mom then shared the dreadful news with me that Brian had died. I was in shock and couldn't believe this was real. I remember thinking, "Things like this happen to *other* people, not to *us*!" In the seconds that followed, my pounding heart began to sink as I tried to comprehend what I had just heard, and I knew that life would *never* be the same again. This is how I found out that Brian didn't survive, and that his funeral had already happened—digesting this news was absolutely crushing.

Eventually, I was given more details about how Brian had died. Because of the trauma to his head from landing on the asphalt, he died upon impact. The Mabeys later told me that CPR was performed, and after about five minutes, his pulse returned. However, after Brian was life-flighted and admitted to the children's hospital, it was discovered that all neural activity in his brain had ceased. There was *no* chance of recovery, and the only thing keeping him alive were the life support machines. My dad was at Brian's side at the children's hospital, but my mom was admitted to the hospital that the rest of us were at, so he called her to discuss Brian's grim condition.

Words could never describe how much sorrow filled my parents' souls as they had to make the heart-wrenching decision to have Brian's life support turned off. This occurred on October 5, 1991, which was the day *after* the accident. My dad couldn't handle being in the room while the support was terminated, as the pain was far too much to bear. The only thing that kept my parents going was knowing they still had their three daughters.

As this was happening, Kristin and I were both in critical condition, fighting for our own lives, while Brian was on his way to the other side. The accident happened on a Friday, and Brian's funeral was held the following Tuesday—four days after his passing. At the time, Kristin and I were nowhere near coherent enough to have been told that Brian had passed, and obviously we were not physically able to attend his funeral.

The aspect of not knowing that Brian had passed, until *after* his funeral, has been extremely difficult for both Kristin and me. It has brought up many feelings—mainly sadness and anger. Funerals can bring a sense of closure, and allow the opportunity to say a final goodbye as you see your loved one for the last time. The fact that Kristin and I didn't get that opportunity has made losing him feel surreal and numbing. Ultimately, there is nothing that could have been done to change the fact that we weren't there—it is what it is. This phrase has become one of my life's mottos regarding things that can't be changed. As hard as life can be and as much as I'd like to change certain aspects of it, the best thing I can do is accept the way it is, and make the best of it.

My sister Erika recalls, "I said goodbye, and I held Brian's hand after they had prepared him for the burial. I remember feeling that it couldn't be him; he looked so different." My mom also said that Brian didn't look like himself. Perhaps it was a blessing that Kristin and I weren't there, but at the same time, it would have been nice to hold his hand one more time. Either way feels like a double-edged sword.

During this time, both of my parents were in a daze. They were grieving the loss of their son while coping with the severe injuries of two of their daughters, including the strong possibility that I wouldn't survive, while doing their best to give Erika the emotional support she needed. As if that weren't enough, my mom also suffered injuries, she no longer had a car, and found herself unexpectedly unemployed. As a result, some information slipped through the cracks regarding my care, including obtaining my hospital records. I never had an advocate keeping track of everything that had happened to me, or noting any recommended actions.

The thought of obtaining my records never dawned on me until 2007, 16 years after the accident, when I realized that I could request them. The records were the answer that would resolve many of my questions, and with one simple phone call, I finally held them in my hands. Up until this point, I only knew what I had been told, and it was about time that I was able to puzzle some pieces back together. At last, I could see the number of surgeries that I had undergone, and the details of the dire condition I had been in so many years ago.

The records unlocked many buried emotions that had been covered in dust for years. As I processed what I was reading, it cleared up a lot of confusion that had been swirling around in my mind for so long, and Google was a much-needed assistant in helping me define all the medical terms. Upon reading through them, I found that the surgeon who worked on my nose had noted the likelihood of needing more work done, which would have been nice to know—it is what it is.

I had always thought that Dr. Mabey held all the answers about my condition, but I realized that although he was the person who could fill in a lot of the blanks regarding what happened at the scene of the accident, ultimately, he was only with us for a total of an hour and a half, because once we were life-flighted, he was no longer involved. Dr. Mabey had told me that when my clavicle broke, it punctured my left lung. But after I read through my records, I found that once I arrived at the hospital, the doctors discovered that the impact of hitting the ground had caused my right lung to collapse. When a lung collapses, a chest tube must be surgically inserted into the pleural space between the lung and chest wall, to re-expand the lung. Ever since the accident, I have noted two surgical scars on both sides, near my ribs, and I've been puzzled as to why there was one on each side, when I had been told that only *one* lung had collapsed. It didn't make sense for so long, and I was disturbed by this mystery surgical scar on my right side, which was identical to the one on my left. Making the discovery that both lungs had collapsed, finally solved that mystery!

3

THE AFTERMATH

Erika's injuries were mostly emotional; however, as the car rolled, she incurred a cut on her scalp, and the sight of blood dripping down her forehead was the first thing she saw once the car stopped rolling. She sat in a daze, slumped over the steering wheel, as she heard screaming coming from outside the car, recalling that, "Everything felt magnified." As she tried to comprehend what had just transpired, she asked my mom, who was still in the seat next to her, "What happened? Was I driving?!" As she began to realize the awful truth, a feeling of devastation consumed her, as her stomach and heart sank to the floor of the car. At that moment, she felt like she wanted to curl up and die. I can't imagine the utter despair and horror that she felt in that moment—and beyond. My heart breaks that my sister suffered this unimaginable trauma.

Erika recalls, "I remember looking in the mirror once I got to the hospital and it looked like I had been beaten by a gang! I remember thinking, 'If I look like this, I can't imagine what everyone else looks like!'" She went on to enter a phase of rebellion and spent years mired in deep guilt. It's taken time, but she has come to a good place. Being the driver—at any age—would be such a difficult position to be in, let alone at just 16-years old. My mom has said "Had I been the driver, I don't know if I could have survived." While the thought of surviving something so daunting is almost unfathomable, we don't truly realize our strengths until we are faced with harsh challenges. Erika is such a strong soul, and my heart goes out to her.

She finished high school, and a few years after the accident, she got married, and is the mother of five children. She has since remarried and is very happy. Through her second marriage, she has gained four bonus children, totaling nine. She loves being a mother, which had always been her dream since she was a little girl. She recently became a grandmother and loves spending time with her little granddaughter. She is also currently in school to become a Licensed Massage Therapist (LMT). Throughout her life, she has always felt a warm energy running through her hands—she truly has a healing touch and was meant to do this work. I love seeing her shine as a mother, grandmother, and soon-to-be LMT.

Kristin suffered from one broken femur, and a hairline fracture in her pelvis on the opposite side. She also incurred a closed head injury, resulting in short-term memory loss, lasting several weeks. Happily, she has made a full recovery. She finished high school and went on to get married and attend college, graduating with her elementary teaching degree. She taught fourth grade for two years, until becoming a mother, and has four children. She eventually became an entrepreneur and opened her own preschool, which she owned, ran, and taught, for several years. She has since divorced and is thriving in her independence. She now teaches first grade, which she excels at and loves—she was truly born to teach. Making a difference in children's lives is her passion and it is so inspiring and amazing to see her doing what brings her so much joy.

My Mom's injuries included a broken clavicle, and a dislocated elbow. Her physical therapist told her that she would never be able to fully extend her arm, but she was determined to completely recover, and with dedication and hard work, she has. During her recovery, she joined a bereavement group for mothers, which helped her tremendously. Since the accident, she has grown to be much more spiritually aware. Her counselor inspired her to eventually become a licensed minister, and as of 2025, she has officiated almost one thousand weddings! Although my mom has been dealt some big lemons in life, she hasn't let them sour her soul. Instead, she has looked for the growth that they can offer and has chosen to turn them into something much sweeter. The accident really guided her towards finding her path and passion in life.

As I mentioned, my dad wasn't in the car with us because my parents had divorced about six years prior. When the accident occurred, my dad was attending a football game at Brigham Young University. My dad and Brian religiously attended every home game that BYU played. Had we not been traveling that weekend, Brian would have been sitting next to my dad, nudging him with his elbow, wanting to borrow the binoculars. Everything was right in the world for my dad that day, *except* for the empty seat next to him.

1988: My dad, 43, and Brian, 6, being silly

As my dad watched the game, he glanced at the giant scoreboard over the north end of the field and his heart dropped when he saw that it was flashing his name, requesting that he immediately report to campus security. He knew that something terrible had happened, and from that moment forward, life would *never* be the same.

As soon as he was told the alarming news, he frantically drove up to Primary Children's Hospital to be at Brian's side. Oblivious to the world around him, horror engulfed his heart as he raced to the hospital, hearing only the sound of his heart pounding and the wind rushing through the car window. Tears of worry ran down his cheeks at the mere thought of losing his *only* son, whom he loved more than life itself, and for whom he had envisioned such a promising future. Nothing will ever replace the loss of his precious son, and he still suffers from a broken heart to this day.

As for Brian, words cannot capture how truly amazing this boy was, or shall I say, *is*, but I will try my best. Brian was everything that a family could ever hope for, especially as the "caboose." After having three daughters, my parents finally got their son, and my sisters and I finally got our brother! Brian was the missing link that livened up our family. He lit up every room that he walked into, and with just one silly look, he would have everyone in complete hysterics. He was handsome, athletic, stylish, mature for his age, and was adored by all who knew him.

His big brown eyes acted as a fishhook, reeling in the attention of girls, and his olive skin was the envy of all who knew him. When he'd flash his bright smile, any chance of saying "no" to him disappeared, no matter what it was that he wanted.

The phone was constantly ringing with calls from his classmates and friends. He would often come to me for advice as to what he should do when multiple friends would invite him to walk to school. How could he choose? How could he let someone down? Such are the dilemmas of a popular nine-year-old boy.

Brian absolutely loved music. Starting at the age of just two years old, he idolized Michael Jackson, and as he grew, his new idols became the New Kids on the Block. He loved chasing seagulls, teasing his sisters, being a Cub Scout, rollerblading, and biking around the neighborhood. He loved sports and was a natural-born athlete.

Brian excelled at every sport he tried, which were many: baseball, basketball, swimming, soccer, golf, and gymnastics. Brian was truly a little superstar, and as you will read, he is also a superstar at sending signs from beyond.

1989: Brian, age seven

1991: Brian, age nine

After having tried so many sports, the next sports adventure that Brian wanted to tackle was little-league football. However, my dad feared letting Brian play football because of the injuries that come as a side-effect of the sport. One day, as father and son discussed the possibility of starting little-league football, my dad lovingly tried to sway Brian's desire, and recalls Brian looking at him and saying "Dad, I can take the pain." Little did my dad realize that it would be him, and all of us, who would have to take the pain. Losing Brian has been painful for us all. We lost the chance to watch Brian continue growing up, to get married, to have children —all the things. Grief encompasses far more than just losing the one you love; it includes the loss of all your dreams for them, and with them.

As for how I am doing, the story continues... My stay in the hospital lasted exactly two weeks: arriving on a Friday, and leaving two Fridays later. From there, I was transferred to Western Rehabilitation Center, in Sandy, Utah, and Kristin joined me there as well. We both needed to be in a wheelchair-accessible facility, and we needed physical and occupational therapy multiple times a day, so it made sense for us to reside there. My memories from the rehab center are a bit sharper than the hospital, but even so, much of the rehab is a blur as well. I was so grateful to have my sister there with me; we were able to share a room, and being together offered us companionship, and brought the pair of us a sense of home.

4

MEMORIES

When I arrived at the rehabilitation center, it was mid-October. Up until my arrival at the rehab, I didn't remember *anything* about the day of the accident. I was transported directly from the hospital to the rehab center, so there was no going home in between the change of facilities. On my way there, I can still remember seeing the tops of the fall-colored trees rushing past, as I laid on the stretcher in the ambulance that would deliver me to my new "home," while wondering what this new place would be like. Kristin had been released from the hospital several days earlier, and spent those days back at our house. However, it quickly became clear to my mom that Kristin was still having some memory issues, so she made the decision to admit Kristin to the rehab, as well.

When I was first brought to our room in the rehab center, Kristin was sitting up in her bed, as she had arrived several minutes earlier. I was wheeled over to the bed that awaited me, and the nurses assisted my transfer into it. Kristin and I both sat there in our beds, staring forward in silence—like zombies. Like I said, up until this point, I didn't have any memories from the *day of* the accident. But as we sat there in our new beds, the memories that *led up to* the accident came rushing back to me, in a flash.

It was extremely surreal to experience these memories all at once, but from my standpoint, this is how they all came flooding back to me... In an instant, I remembered that it had been a clear Friday afternoon in October, and I had just finished my first week as a new student at Salt Lake Community College. I attended school in my hometown, so I lived at home with my mom, sisters, and brother. I drove home from school that day with my windows down, absorbing the invigorating coolness of the air, while listening to the R.E.M. album, *Murmur*, free of concern or worries. To this day, that album brings back memories of a time when things were simple, just before tragedy struck, and is difficult for me to listen to because of the emotions it brings up. Once I arrived home, my mom had already picked up Kristin from school, and asked if I would go pick up Brian and Erika from their schools. All three of them attended different schools: Erika was in high school, Kristin in junior high, and Brian in elementary school.

I went to pick up Brian first, and on my way, I wondered if I'd need to go into the office and check him out. However, when I pulled into the pick-up area, he was already walking towards my car. I look back on this now, and feel it was symbolic of being "his time to go," and that he was ready.

Then, Brian and I picked up Erika, who was out in front of her school with some friends. They had their backs turned to us, and Brian hopped out of the car and snuck up behind them. He grabbed Erika's butt, which he would do to all of us from time to time. She turned around and laughed as they both came giggling to the car. We went home and stuffed the car full of the things we needed for our weekend trip to St. George, Utah, which is approximately a four-hour drive from where we lived in Cottonwood Heights, Utah —a suburb of Salt Lake City. We were going there to support a close family friend who was going to run in the annual St. George Marathon.

I had been struggling with the decision as to whether I should go on this trip or not. Every weekend, my best friend and I would go to a local spot called the Pompadour, where we'd watch bands perform; it was our favorite thing to do, because we shared a love of music. If I went on this trip, I reasoned, I'd forego my weekend ritual. But at the same time, I was feeling nudged to go with my family. I was torn, but ultimately, I decided to skip the music scene that weekend and travel with my family. Time was slipping by, and I thought, "I just started college, and my siblings are growing up so fast. Who knows if I'll ever have this opportunity to go on a trip with all of them again?" So, my decision was made. I've often wondered what life would have been like, had I decided not to go. Even though it almost cost me my life, I am glad that I went because everything I went through has made me who I am today.

1989: My siblings and I: Karin, 16 (bottom left); Kristin, 12 (top left); Erika, 14 (top right); and Brian, 7 (bottom right)

As we were all getting into the car, I was surprised when Erika hopped into the driver's seat. Immediately, worry filled my gut. I didn't think it was a good idea for her to drive all of us, because she was so freshly licensed and we were traveling such a long distance, but I didn't say anything because I wanted to keep the peace. Looking back, I feel as though my soul was speaking through my gut—knowing what was about to take place.

The front seats in our station wagon were equipped with automatic seatbelts, which was a feature that most new cars offered back then. With this, the shoulder belt automatically moves into place upon closing the door after starting the vehicle, leaving the lap belt to be buckled manually. Since my mom and Erika were in the front, they were automatically buckled in, and they also buckled their lap belts. My mom told all of us in the back seats to put our seatbelts on; however, at the time, law didn't require them to be worn. I specifically remember replying with, "Nothing ever happens," and commenting about how seatbelts "aren't comfortable." So unfortunately, I did not wear mine, and neither did Kristin or Brian.

Before we ventured off, we stopped at a nearby gas station to load up on snacks. We all loved Hostess lemon fruit pies, and got several of them, and we each picked out our favorite candy—mine was Reese's Peanut Butter Cups. Once we all had our treats, we were on our way.

As Erika drove along the freeway, my mom coached her on how to use cruise control, which I remember feeling *very* uneasy about. To distract from my anxiousness, I skimmed through the latest teen magazines, while Kristin and Brian leaned in to read the current happenings of the *Beverly Hills 90210* actors. Little did we know, this would be the last time we'd see our little brother.

Brian was obsessed with Jason Priestley's style, who played Brandon Walsh on *Beverly Hills 90210*, and Brian loved to imitate him with the clothes he wore and the way he styled his hair. Brian was a little stud, and wore his pair of Girbaud jeans almost every day, throwing them in the laundry basket as little as possible. He would style them with one of his many cool T-shirts and a pair of the latest sports sneakers that my dad frequently bought for him. Although the memories *leading up* to the accident have now returned, the memories *of* the accident are still locked away somewhere in the unreachable parts of my mind, for which I am grateful.

5

THE REHABILITATION CENTER

As Kristin and I settled into our new home at the rehabilitation center, my favorite holiday, Halloween, was approaching. My dad stopped by to visit one afternoon, with my and Kristin's favorite candy in hand. For me, he had a whole bag of Reese's Mini Peanut Butter Cups. I could hardly wait to eat the chocolate and peanut-buttery goodness, but in an instant, my favorite candy became my least favorite, as nausea swept over me while trying to swallow one. I had been so eager to devour the treat, but even the smell of them repulsed me. Therefore, my visitors ended up leaving with handfuls of them. For the next 10 years, the thought of eating another one couldn't cross my mind, without feeling nauseated. I was puzzled as to why I had such a sudden distaste for them, but I soon realized that a subconscious association between them, and the horrific day of the accident, must have been made. They had been the treat that I chose from the gas station right before we left, and I had been eating them in the car, right before my world was turned upside down.

The first time our mom came to see us in the rehab, she vomited in the bushes before entering the building, as the thought of us living in this place, rather than at home, made her sick to her stomach. Kristin and I had several visitors: family, friends, neighbors, classmates, and even a few of our past teachers. My Aunt Sheila brought me a journal, which gave me an outlet to record my experiences, which is where I wrote my poem, "Emotional Weather."

A friend of mine named Robert came to visit often. I had worked with him, and we attended school together since the sixth grade. Interestingly, the room that Kristin and I were staying in was the same room that he had stayed in approximately one year earlier, while he recovered from a tragic car accident, as well. Robert and I shared the same taste in music, and he brought me a large poster of my favorite band, Depeche Mode, and hung it on the wall next to my bed. This made the room feel less sterile and more like home, as my bedroom at home was basically a tribute to Depeche Mode. Robert would always bring a lot of laughter with him, and his visits really lifted our spirits.

The facility had several whiteboards which listed upcoming outings and activities for the patients, such as going to the park, the mall, or a restaurant. When Kristin and I got stir-crazy, we would wheel ourselves down the hallways to visit the multiple whiteboards that were spread throughout the facility. We'd grab a marker and add additional activities to the boards, such as skydiving and Grateful Dead concerts, and we'd laugh until our stomachs hurt from simply *imagining* the confusion on people's faces as they read these outlandish suggestions. Our time at the rehab was made much more bearable because we were together.

Kristin and I were diligent with our physical therapy twice a day. Just before Thanksgiving, Kristin was allowed to return home once she began using crutches, but I was still wheelchair-bound. After approximately one month without Kristin, I asked if there was any way that I could go home, too.

Being able to go home before I could walk depended upon three things:

1. Strengthening my arms so I could lift myself into my wheelchair from the floor, and scoot up the stairs, using only my arms
2. Making our bathroom wheelchair-accessible by removing the door
3. Obtaining a special showering stool

My mom had someone remove the door, and she purchased the stool that I needed. I worked hard to strengthen my arms, and I was able to get home just before Christmas—it was a Christmas miracle! From then on, my mom would take me to and from physical therapy, once a day. Eventually, my legs could handle bearing weight, and I was able to move from a wheelchair to crutches. Then finally, I learned to walk again. Now it was time for the next phase of my life to begin…

6

HOME AGAIN

Being home was much better than the rehab, but the home I returned to was not the same one I had left—it was so different without Brian there. I often wondered what life would look like, had we all been wearing our seatbelts, like my mom had asked us to. One thing is for sure: ever since the accident, my family and I don't go *anywhere* without wearing them.

When I got home, I found that Brian's belongings had been condensed from a bedroom, down to a box, which felt more like a box of leftover souvenirs. I came to learn that I wasn't the only one to find Brian's belongings this way—the rest of my family did as well. Brian's room had been cleared out by some of our relatives, within just a couple days of the accident. This took place while my mom and Erika were in the hospital, where they stayed for three days following the accident. They were both in such a state of grief that when they try to recount how this was done without their knowledge, it is just a blur. Our relatives' hearts were in the right place, as they wanted to take this burden off my mom's shoulders; however, it really affected our emotional healing, as we all longed to see his room the way he kept it, just one last time. The fact that his room was cleared out without any of us being there evoked many feelings for us—it is what it is

Brian's room was now my sisters', and the posters that once covered his walls, were gone. The opportunity to lay in his bed one last time, put my head on his pillow, and hug his favorite stuffed animals, was gone, too. Yet, the yellowed leaves on the twin sycamores that stood outside our home, remained. That year, they forgot to fall, waiting for the little boy to come and play underneath them—but he never did.

Thankfully, we were able to take a few things from the box, but it felt wrong—almost as if he'd been erased. Nothing feels right once someone you love is gone. In retrospect, perhaps not seeing his room the way he'd left it, safeguarded us from further pain. Just over one year after the accident, I wrote the following description of Brian's room:

THE BEDROOM

The room was not too large, yet it wasn't too small—it was the perfect size for a nine-year-old boy. It was easy to tell that this was the room of a little boy because of the chaos that lived there. Orange shag carpet covered the floor, decorated with sneakers that had run across dozens of grassy fields and skidded across many basketball courts. "New Kids on the Block" posters covered the walls, leaving only a sliver of wall space behind. His bed was occupied by stuffed animals, and toys were scattered throughout. Remnants of his search for "just the right outfit" hung out of the open dresser drawers.

While at school or with friends, a basketball kept his stuffed animals' company, but the minute he got home, it accompanied him outside to shoot hoops. When he wasn't outside, he could often be found in front of his dresser, debating what to wear, or sitting in a clearing on the floor, playing video games. Whenever I'd help him clean, a proud smile would sweep across his face.

On his ninth birthday, his friends were able to witness the rare sighting of his clean room. The carpet was clear, Teenage Mutant Ninja Turtle figurines had found a space on his shelf, and the video game cords were set aside. All his friends enjoyed spending time with him in his room, and looked forward to the next year, but nobody knew that for him, next year wouldn't come.

My two sisters have now moved in, and the chaos that once lived there has moved out. All that remains lives only in our memories. The floor is clear, the Teenage Mutant Ninja Turtles now occupy a box, and the walls where New Kids on the Block posters once hung are now bare. I never thought I'd miss the mess, but I do.

—Karin Bozich, November 1992

Once Kristin and I were settled, we went to visit Brian's grave for the first time. It was disturbing to know that our beloved brother, whom we last saw in the car, was now lying six feet underneath our soles. He had missed Christmas and the New Year, and was soon to miss his next birthday—it just wasn't the same without him. After visiting his grave, we decided to finally watch a recording of Brian's funeral, which we had on a video tape that our Uncle Orin had given us.

Although it would never be the same as attending his funeral, it was as close as we could get. We were thankful that our uncle had been so thoughtful to record it for us. He warned us about the very end of the video, which had Brian resting in his coffin. We appreciated the warning so that we had a choice; we chose not to watch that part. It would have been too strange to see it on tape, and it's not the way we wanted to remember our brother—this was the *only* time we ever watched the video.

When Brian's next birthday arrived, my mom invited all his friends over for cake and ice cream. Afterwards, we all went to his gravesite and released balloons, sang "Happy Birthday," and shared our favorite memories of him. It was very special and meant a lot to us to have all his friends together in one place. Although Brian wasn't there in body, we could all feel him there in spirit.

7

HEALING

I returned to college a few months after my arrival home. During this time, I walked with a limp, which made the walk across campus a bit longer than before. Around June of 1992, about eight months after the accident, my limp finally dissipated. It had improved so gradually that I hadn't even noticed, until a friend pointed it out to me. Realizing this helped me see how far I'd come, and it was such a great feeling.

Around August of 1992, the one-year anniversary of the accident was drawing near, and the plate under my left eye began to shift, which caused me to have double vision when I became tired. Luckily, it was able to be corrected with surgery, and I am so thankful that my vision is better. Even so, my left eye doesn't sit quite the same as the other eye, and my nose still deviates to the left, even after multiple surgeries.

Because I struck the ground on my left side, I have some slight nerve damage on the left side of my face, which makes it not quite as responsive as the right side. Although it may not be very noticeable to others, it is like a glaring light to me, especially when I see myself on video.

The nerve damage also affected my left shoulder, causing permanent muscle atrophy and partial numbness. Because of the damage, my shoulder slopes inward and aches during certain activities, or when I'm under stress. It will never be as strong as the other shoulder, but I've been able to strengthen the muscles around it. When I see pictures of myself with my shoulder exposed, I often vow never to wear sleeveless tops again.

These physical changes have caused me some grief over the years, as change is a form of loss. Not only do I grieve Brian, but I also grieve my previous self. Grief never fully dissolves, but I have finally reached a good place—most of the time. In the past when I'd find myself focusing on these changes, guilt would take a seat next to me. It would tell me that because I survived and Brian didn't, I had no right to be bothered about the way my appearance has changed. I would suppress my emotions, telling myself that I should just feel lucky to be alive, and that I'm lucky to even have a face, nose, eyes, vision, arms, and legs.

With time, I've found that grieving the loss of who I was before my injuries is just as important as grieving the loss of Brian. All feelings are valid and it's alright to give myself the space and the grace to fully feel the mixed emotions of grief, sadness, anger, and guilt, and I know that Brian is right there beside me while I'm feeling them.

It can feel overwhelming when these emotions intermingle, as every emotion is eager to be expressed. I have found healing by allowing each one to take their turn, and holding space for myself to fully feel them, rather than dismiss them. By doing this, I've come to accept my physical changes, yet at times, these feelings can resurface, but when they do, I face them and then let them go—and *then* I turn to gratitude.

Shifting my focus to gratitude has helped me in my healing journey, and I've found that no matter what, I can always find something to be grateful for. During my and Kristin's stay in the hospital and rehab, there were many others who were a lot worse off than we were, including some who would never walk again.

Gratitude changes everything, and when I choose to focus on it, anything that bothers me about my physical changes quickly vanish. Having gratitude is truly a superpower: it can take you from a dark place and lift you up into the light—just as a superhero would.

During the months I lived at the rehab center, I remember sitting in my bed and seeing something on the shelf across the room that I wanted. It was frustrating because I could no longer just get up and grab it, because completing simple tasks now took much more effort. It really put into perspective how much we take for granted each day, and developing this new viewpoint has allowed me to turn my frustration into something positive, giving me a new outlook on life. For example, the second we stub our toe, we're suddenly grateful for how it was feeling two seconds prior. But before that, gratitude for a pain-free toe never even crossed our minds. There is always something that could be ailing you, that isn't, and there is always something to be grateful for. Take a minute to be grateful for all the things in your life—right down to your toes.

The practice of loving myself unconditionally has helped me immensely. I used to have a lot of negative self-talk, but one day I thought about how I'd feel if a friend were to say those things to me, and I froze—realizing how badly I was treating myself. So, I made a commitment to myself to quit being my own worst enemy, and I began being my own best friend. This has been instrumental in helping me accept my physical changes and truly love myself. Of course, there are things about my appearance that bother me, but the difference now is that I don't dwell on the negatives—I focus on the positives instead. Adopting this habit has helped me become much kinder to myself than I used to be.

For years, I was very self-conscious about my scars, but I've chosen to look at them through a new lens and wear them proudly.

I have realized that although sometimes the things we don't like about ourselves can seem large in our own eyes, they are small to the people who love us; they only see the light that's in our eyes.

In the spring of 1993, the rods in my legs had performed their duty, and they've now found a home in a vase that sits on my office bookcase. I was so happy to stand on my own again, and that I had finally reached a point where most of my recovery was now behind me. It felt *so* good!

8

RELIGION + SPIRITUALITY

I was raised in a religious home and was a very good rule follower. I was active in my church and engaged in scripture study throughout my teenage years. While I was living in the rehab, my mom mentioned that they held church there on Sundays. I was excited to hear that, and Kristin and I attended the next service.

During the service, as I sat there in my wheelchair, I was surprised to find that I felt numb inside—like something that had once been there, was now gone. Although I was devout, there were some teachings of the church that had never resonated with me, and I was finding that those teachings made even less sense to me now. The accident acted as a catalyst, causing me to re-evaluate my beliefs, which put me on a trajectory of self-discovery. Losing Brian, and later receiving signs from him, sent me on a path to spiritual awakening.

By coming so close to death, I realized that I had never truly lived. This realization was a defining moment—I was ready to start living my life and making my own choices. I knew that we came to Earth to gain experiences, learn from our choices, and grow through them, and I felt that I never really had that opportunity, because I had always followed such a straight line. It's not that I wanted to go out and start breaking the rules, but I wanted the *freedom* to choose.

I searched deep within my soul, asking, "What if I hadn't followed such a straight line—would I be separated from Brian, had I died?" My religion taught that families can be together forever—but *only* if certain ordinances and covenants are kept. As I continued soul-searching, I came to see that, for me, these teachings were grounded more in fear and obedience than in love and freedom. I recognized that whether I continued in my religion, or not, that my family and I would be together again. Our Creator holds *unconditional* love for all of us, just a parent does for their child. Unconditional love is just that—we are loved no matter what and will *always* be welcomed home with open arms. So, I began on the journey of carving my own path, rather than following the path that my religion had laid out for me—and like a snake that sheds its skin, I shed my religion.

Losing your religion is like a death—the death of who you were and what you believed. Once I stopped attending church, I discovered that it's much more difficult to create your own path than it is to follow one. Instead, you must figure out what *you* believe—and don't believe. Although religion had been part of my life since the beginning, it was like a switch had been flipped—changing my entire outlook. With a renewed vision, I saw that religion and spirituality don't always go hand in hand. Some people are religious but not spiritual, whereas other people are spiritual and not religious. Spirituality comes from *inside* oneself, not from an *outside* source, such as religion.

I never attended the church service in the rehab center again. Once I returned home, with encouragement from my mom, I went to church a handful of times, but never made it to a second handful. I still felt an emptiness inside, as though something were missing. Because of my lack of attendance, I soon became the black sheep of my family. However, my mom witnessed my newfound freedom, and within a couple of years, she was inspired to try a different church. She loves the community and structure that religious organizations offer, so she began attending Unity Spiritual Center, which is a non-denominational religion that doesn't subscribe to a specific set of doctrines or rituals. She has been enjoying their services ever since. My dad stopped participating in church not long after the accident, and is happy without religion in his life. Both of my sisters remained active in the church for the following 20 years.

A person's religious or spiritual beliefs don't matter to me; "to each their own" is my philosophy, as I feel that there are many paths that lead to the same destination. I respect that the structure of religion works for many, but it doesn't work for me. I know both religious and non-religious people who have received signs from their loved ones, and I feel if that really mattered, it would only be one-sided.

My church is now within, and I believe that what's most important is what's inside your heart. It's about how you behave—not what you believe.

NEAR-DEATH EXPERIENCES

I wanted to find out where Brian went and where we're all eventually going. Losing him sparked my curiosity in studying near-death experiences (NDEs), which are experiences related to a life-threatening situation that are recounted by a person after briefly experiencing clinical death, followed by a return to consciousness, or after being in critical condition where death was conceivable. Eventually, my studies helped me identify my own NDE.

While NDEs differ from person to person, many of them share common elements such as observing one's own body from above, seeing a bright light, traveling through a tunnel, being enveloped in an inexplicable amount of love, encountering spiritual beings, and gaining a vast understanding of how the Universe works.

There is a recurring theme in many NDE's, which experiencers call a "life review" in which every interaction they've ever had during their life—both positive and negative—is experienced from the other person's perspective. This reminds me of the Golden Rule, which states, "Do unto others as you would have them do unto you." Depending on how you treated others, the life review will either feel like Heaven or Hell.

Experiencers have said that we do not face judgement, other than our own, but the impact of feeling how we made others feel becomes either our reward or our punishment. Once you experience the effect that you had on others, your lesson is learned, and you are changed because of it. I love studying NDEs, and learning about them has really helped me along my spiritual path.

SPIRITUALITY

My guiding principles are to do the things that lift my soul, light me up, and bring me joy. By living my life in this way, I feel uplifted, connected to the other side, and closer to Brian. I have felt Brian everywhere, and I've even received messages in a smoke-filled dive bar, as you will discover as you read on. Because of this, I know that it doesn't matter whether you go shopping on Sundays, sit in a church, climb a mountaintop, or hang out in a bar—we can connect to Spirit no matter where we are.

Becoming spiritual didn't happen right away; it took some time and some life lessons before I really grew into my spirituality. The signs and experiences I share here have greatly contributed to this growth. Not only can we receive signs and guidance from our loved ones, but we can also receive them from a divine energy. This energy consists of *all things heavenly,* and depending upon a person's beliefs, this energy may be referred to by many different names: God, Heavenly Father, Divinity, The Universe, Source, Creator, Higher Power, All That Is, Spirit Guides, and Guardian

Angels. Throughout this book I will be using the term "Divine Spirit," to refer to this energy.

We are all made of this energy, and because of that, I am choosing to include loved ones *and* the Higher Self, as part of Divine Spirit. Our loved ones include deceased relatives and friends who we knew *during* this life, plus ancestors and friends who we knew *before* this life (whom we have temporarily forgotten), including future generations. The heavenly energies of Divine Spirit can work together as a team, or individually to communicate to us by way of signs. Even though we cannot see this energy, it does exist; it simply vibrates at a higher frequency, which is invisible to the physical eye.

When we receive a sign, sometimes we know exactly who it's from because it's specific to a certain loved one—their song, their number, their smell, etc. Yet other times, many assumptions could be made as to who it's from, such as, "Was this sign from God, my Higher Self, Grandma, an ancestor, or my Guardian Angel?" So, the expression "Divine Spirit" incorporates all this divine energy.

The Higher Self is the highest state of our own consciousness—it is the soul. It is the larger, enlightened part of each of us that *simultaneously* exists in the higher realm. The movie *Avatar* is a great example of the relationship between the Higher Self and the earthly self. In this film, the main character's body stays in an enclosed capsule on a spaceship, while his consciousness is transferred into an avatar where he can simultaneously experience life on a planet. Similarly, our Higher Selves stay on the other side, but just a *portion* of our consciousness gets transferred into our "avatars" to experience life on Earth.

Because only a portion is transferred, we only have access to a small fraction of the knowledge and wisdom that the entirety of our consciousness holds. Otherwise, we wouldn't be able to learn the lessons that life offers. It would be like trying to play the game "pin the tail on the donkey" without a blindfold, which would be pointless. But we can tap into *some* of this wisdom by quieting our minds, being present, and meditating. Our Higher Selves can reach out to us when we need guidance by giving us little nudges disguised as intuition (felt in the heart), instincts (felt in the gut), and inspiration (thoughts that arise in your mind that aren't your own). Once we leave our bodies, we integrate back into the *full* wisdom that our Higher Selves hold, becoming whole and enlightened once again, as our memories from that in which we came, also return.

Up until the accident, I prayed to the God whom my religion had taught me about since I was a child. However, once I shed my religious skin, my idea of God began to shift from a man sitting on a throne within the pearly gates of heaven, to an energy that has a distinct essence of its own, while also encompassing everything in unison. When I pray now, I direct my intention to the essence that I envision as my Creator, while also viewing this sacred time as an open meeting where the other heavenly energies of Divine Spirit are welcome to join—if their help is needed. I see prayer as a way of being able to thank any of these divine energies and ask them for help, in an all-encompassing way. The power of prayer is real. When we are in trouble, or have fallen away from our intended path, Divine Spirit can take the initiative to assist us, but for our day-to-day issues, Divine Spirit usually won't interfere—unless we ask. When we ask for help, we are giving permission to receive the help we need.

In my prayers of the past, I would state out each word in my mind, as if I were speaking. My prayers became so routine that I began to feel as if I were reciting a poem. But, as I've come to understand more about the afterlife, I now pray using *more heart* and *less words*. On the other side, communication is done by telepathy, which is based on feelings rather than words, so I try and do the same in my prayers, which end up being mostly quiet moments of deep gratitude and sincere emotions.

During my time of prayer, I always welcome being used as an instrument for good in this world, asking to be guided to where I'm needed. Therefore, I try to be perceptive as I go about my days and follow any inspiration that I receive. Sometimes it's as simple as having the feeling to offer someone food, and it turns out that they had either not been feeling well or wondering what to do for dinner, or I will feel the need to reach out to someone who ended up really needing to connect.

When I ask a loved one for a sign, it is different from a prayer. I direct my intention towards that specific loved one, and I consider it an invitation. In this life, we ask the people we love for help all the time, and just because a loved one is now in spirit, it doesn't mean that we can't ask them for guidance and signs—they are still right here; we just can't see them.

9

SPIRITUALLY TRANSFORMATIVE EXPERIENCES

PRE-BIRTH MEMORY

I've always had a deep knowing that there's much more to life than we realize. I attribute this to a mental image that I've carried with me before I ever took my first breath. It has anchored me in knowing that my existence didn't just begin the day I was born. Years ago, I wrote the following journal entry about it:

> "When I was about 11 years old, I came to my mother with something that I wasn't sure how to explain. I told her that I held a memory—a snapshot in time that had been with me since the beginning, but I didn't know where it came from. It was a view from above, looking down upon a woman with dark hair that was piled on top of her head. She was sitting at a desk while typing and I could see the tops of her shoulders. The woman was wearing a pastel-colored shirt or dress but the color wasn't lavender, nor was it light pink—it was a distinct mixture of the two. The flooring consisted of large square tiles that were white with black speckles.

When I shared this with my mother, her jaw dropped, as I had just described the office where she worked as a secretary, when she was pregnant with me. She said I described the flooring perfectly, and that she used to pull her hair up into a beehive hairdo. She also had a dress in the exact color that I had described, which she wore before becoming pregnant, and during the early stages of her pregnancy with me.

I was never quite sure what this memory was, until I finally shared it with my mother. I now know that this was an actual memory—from *before* I was born. I have since learned that the formal name for this type of experience is a 'pre-birth memory,' and I feel especially lucky that I was able to keep this special memory, which is still just as clear today. I know that I chose my mother, and I am so grateful that she's mine. We have always had a very close and special connection."

This memory I hold dear, and because of it, I have always trusted that if I existed before I entered my body, then surely, I will continue to exist after I exit my body. Although I had no other personal experiences to confirm the existence of something more—I believed.

I have always sensed that I held additional pre-birth memories, but the only one that remained was seeing my mother from above. When I was a child, I screamed a lot—very loudly and angrily. So much so, that my mother turned to my pediatrician multiple times, seeking an explanation, but none could ever be found. It's not in my nature to be angry, and I intuitively feel that I remembered where I came from and what it was like to be free, living in spirit, and I was angry because I was now bound inside of this body, and I wanted to go back. This brings me back to the law of conservation of energy, that says energy only changes form and can neither be *created* nor *destroyed*, which reinforces my belief that I existed before I came here.

I was so loud, that my Uncle Orin nicknamed me S.K. ("Screaming Kid"), and even the neighbors across the street could hear me screaming from inside their home. During my fits of rage, my mom would splash a small glass of water into my face, which would induce crying rather than screaming. My screaming fits stopped around the age of four, and I became extremely quiet and shy. My theory is that a belief had been created within me: it's not okay to express my feelings, and being quiet is preferred. My mom didn't realize the effect of what she was doing, and I hold no anger towards her for that, but once again—it is what it is.

VISITATION EXPERIENCE

During my time in the hospital and rehab, I never felt Brian's presence or received any signs from him. Perhaps he hadn't given me any, perhaps I was too focused on my recovery, or maybe I simply wasn't ready. Whatever the case, in March of 1992, about two months after my return home, I was driving one evening, and I suddenly sensed Brian's distinct presence in the passenger seat, right next to me. I'd never felt a spirit's presence before, but I clearly knew that it was Brian. This visitation experience was spiritually transformative for me, because it showed me that he still exists. This reinforced my belief, rooted in my pre-birth memory, that if we exist before we enter our bodies, we also exist after we exit them. Feeling Brian's presence deepened that belief. As tears ran down my face, I spoke out loud and expressed how much I missed him, and I thanked him for coming to see me. It felt *so* good to feel him close again! His presence lingered for a couple of minutes, and then he was gone...but as you will see in the pages to follow, he isn't truly gone.

OUT OF BODY EXPERIENCE

Around this same time, I had an amazing experience during the middle of the night. I suddenly awoke feeling happier than I have ever felt in my entire life. I wasn't groggy in the slightest; I was bright-eyed and wide awake.

I found myself filled with the most profound sense of pure love and overwhelming joy—it was literally heartwarming! This magnified love set my soul alight with what felt like all the love and happiness that had ever existed—it was love on steroids! Although I wasn't left with the *memory* of the experience, I was left with the *feeling* of it. It was so intense that it was extremely difficult to resist the powerful urge to get out of bed and wake my mom and sisters to tell them how much I loved them. Although it was not easy, I did manage to contain myself and I finally fell back to sleep as the expansive feeling of love began to subside.

The next morning, I shared this with my mom, and we both felt certain that I had some type of mystical experience, which we assumed was most likely with Brian. But, because I didn't remember it, we'll never know for sure. What I do know is that the happiness I felt when I awoke was more than I've ever felt before—or since. I eventually researched what are often described as mystical experiences—visitation dreams, near-death experiences (NDEs), and out-of-body experiences (OBEs)—hoping to find answers. In many of these experiences, people describe feeling such an immense amount of love that it's difficult to put into words. Because of how I felt that night, I could relate—but what exactly had I experienced?

Visitation dreams are vivid and memorable, yet I only recalled the feeling of love I was left with. NDEs and OBEs often overlap, as both involve being outside the body. They also aren't always remembered, since detachment from the body can sometimes disrupt the normal memory encoding process. The difference is the cause: NDEs are related to life-threatening situations, whereas

OBEs can occur spontaneously, often during other states of consciousness such as sleep or meditation. This aligned with my experience, and the way I felt upon waking reflects what many describe during OBEs. That's the explanation that resonates most with me.

NEAR-DEATH EXPERIENCE

Many years after the accident, a memory returned to me. It didn't return all at once—it took time to truly unfold. Over the years, I've come to embrace this memory as an NDE. I believe this experience occurred just before or as I was ejected from the car—the only time I've faced a sudden, life-threatening situation. In moments of extreme trauma, the spirit may separate from the body in search of relief.

In this experience, I was suspended in a vast, pitch-black darkness that seemed to have no beginning and no end. In that silent, comforting space—time stood still. Cradled in the quiet darkness, I was rescued from the chaos and pain surrounding my body.

I felt as though I were just a pair of eyes floating in a strange, empty space—like an outer space without stars. Fully present and immersed in what felt like pure consciousness, I was flooded with a universal knowing—*Ohhh, so this is what it's really all about!* It was a *remembering*—like catching a glimpse behind the scenes of something I had long forgotten.

Although this knowing didn't stay with me, I remember it as something simple, yet profound. It gave me a strong desire to return and likely played a role in how hard I fought to stay alive.

I began to wonder if I had experienced an NDE, yet it didn't align with the most commonly reported elements. As I continued my research, however, I found others who described a sense of universal knowing while floating in a vast, dark nothingness—what they call "the void," where time seemed to disappear.

Hearing these stories validated my experience—my uncertainty began to lift, and I no longer felt alone.

Some people describe rushing through a dark tunnel during their NDE. Perhaps if I had begun moving through that space, it might have felt that way—but I remained still, suspended in the stillness. Given the intensity of the situation and the severity of my injuries, it's no wonder my spirit sought solace in that space. I've come to view the void as a kind of "time out"—a holding place between worlds.

The delayed realization of my NDE made it difficult to process and accept. I was also under the impression that a person needed to clinically die to have an NDE. Although my pulse was barely detectable upon admission to the hospital, I was never pronounced dead. Eventually, I learned that flatlining isn't a prerequisite for an NDE and I was finally able to understand what I'd experienced.

Our memories work in mysterious ways. My mind has locked away much of the trauma from the accident, along with portions of my hospital stay and rehabilitation. Yet over time, the memory of my NDE gradually returned, bringing with it a deeper understanding. I've come to accept that even though it surfaced slowly, it is no less real.

NDEs often carry aftereffects—heightened sensitivity, greater compassion, deeper empathy, intuitive awareness, and spiritual shifts that can draw people away from organized religion and toward a more personal spirituality. I've experienced these too.

I'm grateful that this memory has returned over time. I've come to understand that there is far more to this reality than meets the eye—that our consciousness continues, and that love is what it's all about. This brings me great comfort, and my hope is that you may find the same.

PART II

SIGNS FROM BRIAN

When we lose a loved one, we can lose hope, and our light can be lost. However, once we realize that our loved ones still exist, our dark days can become brighter. There so many types of signs that our departed loved ones can send us. When we receive signs, we finally see that the ones we've lost are never truly gone. This insight can restore our hope and help us find our light again. As you experience these communications from your loved ones, you'll begin to recognize that each and every sign is a brand-new experience that you're having with your loved one—a means of continuing your relationship in a new way.

When signs are unsolicited and happen unexpectedly, they are referred to as After-Death Communications or ADCs, but you can also *ask* your loved ones for signs. Regardless of how they are labeled, communications from the other side are *all* considered signs.

Signs can appear anywhere: in person, on a screen, or in print. One of the most common ways is symbolically—through *objects*: coins and feathers, or through *nature*: animals, birds, insects (usually butterflies, dragonflies, and ladybugs), and rainbows.

Music is also a method through which we can receive signs and messages, such as hearing our loved one's favorite song, especially on a significant date, or when the lyrics of a song seem to be speaking to you. Our loved ones on the other side can somehow orchestrate when and where a certain song will play. They can also make their presence known through visitations or visions. Sometimes you will simply feel their presence, and at other times, you will see your loved one—either while awake, asleep, or in your "mind's eye."

Connecting with our loved ones, through signs, gives us those "wow moments" that feel truly magical. Over the years, my family, friends, and I have received some amazing signs from Brian and other loved ones, which confirm to us that they are still with us. I share these experiences to inspire you with hope, knowing that you can receive signs as well, and that our loved ones continue on—just in a different form. And, if our loved ones do, then surely, we will as well.

10

DROPS OF WATER

In March of 1993, almost a year and a half after the accident, I arrived home from school, and as soon as I walked in the door, my mom began excitedly telling me that she had received a sign from Brian. She had been talking on the phone with her brother (my Uncle Orin), while doodling on a piece of paper. Out of nowhere, one single drop of water landed on the piece of paper, and she looked up in complete and utter bewilderment. She told Orin what had just happened, and his response was that she needed a roof replacement. My mom explained that the roof had been replaced the year before, and the only explanation she could come up with was that the drop of water was a sign from Brian.

I was very skeptical about what she was sharing with me, and I thought, "How could a drop of water be a sign?" but I did my best to be supportive. I asked her if there happened to be a glass of water nearby, or anything that could have caused this to occur. She verified that there was nothing but the pen and paper on the table. I shrugged my shoulders, and while I was sensitive to her beliefs, I didn't believe it was a sign. I had never experienced any physical signs from the other side, so I really didn't know what to think—until it happened to me.

Not long after my mom's experience, I received my first tangible sign, which led me to wholeheartedly believe that what had happened to my mom was, indeed, a sign from Brian.

I was hanging out in my bedroom and noticed that a collage I had made for one of my graphic design classes was coming unglued near the edges. So, I grabbed my glue stick, crisscrossed my legs, and sat down in the middle of the floor to salvage my art.

As I sat and glued, home alone in my bedroom, one single drop of water landed directly in the center of my collage! I looked up, just as my mom had done when it had happened to her. My disbelief instantaneously morphed into belief! I quickly looked back down at the collage, to make sure the drop was still there, or if it was just my mind playing tricks on me. Indeed, it was there, so I touched it. It was wet, but was quickly fading before my eyes.

In that moment, I knew without a doubt that what I had just experienced was a sign from Brian—*my* sign from Brian! He was confirming to me that my mom's sign was from him, that this sign was from him, and to *believe* it. From that moment forward, I was convinced that signs were a real thing, and that life continues after death. I could hardly wait to tell my mom that the same thing had happened to me.

When you hear other people's experiences, just like when I heard my mom's, it's human nature to question and come up with other possible explanations. Rather than a sign, it can be easier to think that it is simply a coincidence, or that the person is subconsciously searching for things to help themselves feel better. Some of these experiences are so mind-blowing that it can be difficult to truly believe—until it happens to you.

This book is filled with true stories, and I encourage you to have an open mind about them and about receiving signs for yourself—and when you get them, you just might become a believer, too. Perhaps you won't, but the choice is yours. I am not here to convince you; I am just here to share these experiences, and you get to decide what *you* believe.

Many years after my mom and I had our experiences with the water, a close friend of mine named Liz, lost her mom to cancer in 2008. It had been about a month since Liz's mom passed, and she and I were out running errands together. As we were getting into her car, she exclaimed, "What the...? A drop of water just landed on my arm, and there's not a cloud in sight!" It was about six o'clock in the evening, during the summer, and the sky was a clear, twilight blue. I immediately knew what had just happened, and I exclaimed, "That drop of water is a sign from your mom!"

I then shared what my mom and I had experienced with the drops of water, and she was amazed and brought to tears, knowing that her mom had just given her a sign, too. Our loved ones can work together on the other side to bring us signs. If Liz had been alone when this had happened, she probably would have shaken her head, not recognizing it as a sign. There couldn't have been a better way for her mom to let her daughter know that she is still with her in spirit, than to send her a drop of water while she was with me. I am sure that Liz's mom knew that I'd recognize this sign, and that she enlisted the help of Brian to deliver it. I could just picture them collaborating to come up with this way of grabbing our attention. It was an incredible experience that I will always remember, and I am sure that Liz will, too.

Drops of water seem to drip into my life at the times I'm least expecting them...

When I was 11 years old, I was diagnosed with mitral valve prolapse, which is when the valve located between the left heart chambers doesn't fully close, causing blood to leak backward across the valve. Ever since being diagnosed, I'd been told that open heart surgery would eventually be necessary.

Every year I would have a checkup with my cardiologist, and every five years an echocardiogram would be performed. My condition caused random heart palpitations, which would either cause my heart to randomly skip a few beats, or start beating extremely fast, for about 10-20 seconds per episode. When it would beat fast, I'd panic and wonder if it would ever find its way back to a normal beat pattern, but it always did. Although I was used to these episodes, they were always a bit startling.

As I entered my late twenties, my annual appointments became semiannual appointments, and the echocardiograms became more frequent. Luckily, the accident hadn't impacted my heart, even though a possible rupture was of concern upon my initial arrival at the hospital. However, in 2002 (11 years after the accident), a new symptom occurred: my heart randomly began to pound, very heavily, as if I were running a marathon, and this would occur whether relaxing or active, and was happening more and more often.

I underwent some testing, and it was confirmed that my valve was now leaking more than it had been a few years ago, and that my heart had slightly enlarged. Even so, my cardiologist said that surgery was not necessary at this point, and it wouldn't be until I began huffing and puffing from simply going up a staircase. I envisioned the scenario in my mind, and I didn't want the anxiety of waiting for that day to come—I wanted to do something about it *now*.

My new symptoms were frightening, and I wanted to put the looming, inevitable surgery behind me. Fate was not going to make this decision—I was. I then heard a message in my mind that said, "Do it now, and it will be repaired." I heard this repeatedly, and it held hands with a sense of urgency that was undeniable. I truly believe that Divine Spirit was guiding me to get this taken care of before things worsened.

However, the cardiology community prefers that women with mitral valve prolapse are done having children before undergoing surgery. The reason for this is because the patient must decide between two valve replacements in the case that the affected valve is not repairable, and each affects a woman's ability to have more children. The first option is to use a pig's valve, which must be replaced every six years, thus requiring repeated open-heart surgeries; this timeline may affect a woman's choice to have more children. The second option requires a mechanical valve, which necessitates the daily and lifelong use of strong blood thinners, which can cause birth defects—eliminating the option of having more children.

The random pounding was nerve-racking, and it began happening more frequently, so I finally surrendered to the message that was repeating in my mind, and I called my cardiologist's office. However, when I asked to speak with him, his nurse was acting as gatekeeper. I explained what was going on, and that I'd recently worn a monitor along with having undergone numerous tests, and that I was ready to have the surgery. But, she insisted that I wear a monitor for two weeks before the option of surgery could even be discussed. She informed me that all the monitors were checked out for the following two weeks—which would put me a month out before I could get any traction. The only option she offered was to wait for a monitor, even though I'd recently worn one. I simply wanted to speak with my cardiologist because he knew what had been happening, but she would not allow it.

I was frustrated with her insistence that I jump through hoops that didn't need to be jumped through. Later that evening, a thought that was not my own popped into my head: "Call after hours!" I thought, "Good idea!" and called the after-hours number that night. I told them what was going on, and that I needed to speak with my cardiologist. Within a few minutes, my doctor personally returned my call. I don't doubt for a single second that the thought had come from Divine Spirit. I explained to my cardiologist that my new symptoms were happening more often, and I felt that I'd have a better chance of valve repair if the surgery was done sooner rather than later. He agreed, and I was scheduled for surgery two weeks later.

Once I had a surgery date, I felt very content about my decision, but there was one more decision knocking at my door...*if* my valve was not repairable, I had to choose which type of replacement I wanted. I couldn't fathom choosing the pig's valve and having to go through open heart surgery every six years. Plus, after all my body had been through with the accident, making the choice of a mechanical valve was a no-brainer. I was 29, single, had no desire for children, and I knew that I could always adopt if I were to change my mind. I felt extremely secure with my decision to have the mechanical valve, if needed, but...I felt certain that my valve would be repaired.

As time inched closer to my surgery date, which was scheduled for late June 2002, I didn't grow nervous until the night before. I was instructed to wash my chest with a special antibacterial soap before going to bed. As I poured the liquid soap into my hands and glided it across my chest, the nerves in my body began to awaken as I thought about the fact that the very next morning, my chest would be cut open, creating one more battle wound to be proud of.

As the sun rose, my nerves followed suit, and like a conductor in an orchestra, they directed my teeth to chatter and my body to shake. When I was taken into the operating room, the cold temperatures amplified my shaking so much that if a passerby had seen me, they would have thought I was seizing. Before I could blink, there was an IV in my arm and I was instructed to count backwards from 10, and upon reaching seven, I was out!

My parents patiently waited, and when I awoke, I immediately asked them if my valve had been repaired, and the answer was a resounding *yes*. It was a moment of absolute relief—for all of us! I know that I had been divinely guided, and I am so grateful that I was open and trusting enough to follow that guidance. Now, all I had to do was recover.

Having my surgery over with was more than a relief, and afterwards I discovered that the timing was essential: my employment, health insurance, and schooling all hinged on having my surgery done sooner rather than later. It's no wonder that I kept hearing that message. Since my surgery, my cardiologist raves that my valve repair was one of the best he's seen. I have no restrictions, leaving me free to do the things I want to do.

Several years later, I went to see a spiritual psychic, specifically seeking information on some health issues, which were not heart-related. The medium told me that she sensed something about my heart, so I shared that my valve had been repaired. She then said that if I hadn't had the surgery when I did, I would have died. Who knows if that would have been the case, but nevertheless, I did find it interesting.

As I've mentioned, motherhood had never been on my radar. My sisters had many children by the time I was in my early thirties, and following in their footsteps wasn't something I wanted to do; I just couldn't envision taking that route. Family and friends would tell me that my biological clock was ticking, but I didn't pay them any heed. However, to my great surprise, the desire for children eventually did find me. I am extremely happy to say that just over a year after my heart surgery, at age 30, I met my husband Shane in the summer of 2003, and we now have two amazing teenagers (a son named Ever, and a daughter named Sola). I absolutely love being a mother. My kids are the sun that lights my world, and motherhood is the greatest joy of my life.

When my kids were around the ages of eight and six, in June of 2017, we were at the store standing in line at the cash register. The cashier noticed the top of my long vertical scar that goes down my chest and asked me about it, so I told her that I'd had open heart surgery. She then slightly lowered her shirt, revealing a scar that looked just like mine. We discovered that we both had been diag-nosed with the same heart condition, had the same surgery, and were both lucky enough to have had our valves repaired! It was so amazing to meet another woman who had walked a similar path. We said goodbye, and my kids and I headed to the car.

As we made our way to the car, time seemed to suddenly move in slow motion as a realization hit me: I had come *so* close to the possibility of not having my kids! The gamble I'd taken by choosing the mechanical valve was such a close call, and I am so glad that I won, because otherwise, they wouldn't be here. With this realization, my heart began to fill with overwhelming gratitude for my miracle children, for a successful surgery, and for listening to and following the guidance that urged me to have it done when I did. I truly feel the guidance came from Divine Spirit.

Right after this moment of realization, things began moving in real-time again. My heart continued filling with gratitude as my son Ever exclaimed, "One drop of water just landed on my head!" I reached over and touched the top of his head, and there was a wet spot. The sky was clear, and immediately I knew that Brian had sent that drop of water! I had previously told my kids about the experiences that my mom and I had had with the drops of water, and I was so happy that my son was able to experience his own "drop of water" sign, firsthand, and that my daughter could also witness it. This drop of water sign was the cherry on top of all the signs with drops of water, as it signified to me that I had made the right choice with having the surgery done when I did. I've often wondered, "Why drops of water?" Perhaps they're not drops of water at all, but tears from Heaven—a way of saying, I miss you, too."

Since these occurrences, I have found that my family and I are not alone in experiencing water droplets as a phenomenon, as there are various spiritual and cultural beliefs that water droplets are signs from higher powers; however, it is not a very common sign. Those who have received these drops of water feel it is other-worldly, associating it with Spirit making itself known. In the experiences my family and I have had, we feel the drops of water came from Brian and have felt distinctly comforted upon receiving them.

11

BRIAN'S SONGS

Music is one of the most common ways that our loved ones can communicate with us from the other side. When you hear a song that reminds you of them, it is often their way of saying hello.

Sometimes the lyrics of a song communicate a message that you needed to hear, almost as if your loved one is speaking directly to you. The songs are generally given on a significant date, if you've asked for a sign, or as you are thinking of your loved one.

Most of the signs that my family and I have received from Brian have been through music. There are a handful of songs which my family and I have come to recognize as "Brian's Songs," most of which were current around the time of Brian's death, in 1991. Whenever we hear any of them, Brian's image practically flashes before our eyes.

"SOMEWHERE OUT THERE"

The song "Somewhere Out There," by Linda Ronstadt and James Ingram, feels very special to us because of its poignant message and because it was sung by family friends at Brian's funeral.

Family, friends, and I have received so many "Somewhere Out There" signs from Brian, like my mom hearing it play on the anniversary of the accident while at a restaurant, or my dad hearing it play amid all the other songs that played on his smart speaker the night before Brian's birthday one year. I just picture all these happenings as little hellos from Brian, and these heavenly greetings hold us over until we can meet again.

I mentioned earlier that Brian was a little stud—even at just nine years old, he had a girlfriend. Her name was Nicole, and she lived across the street from us. Nicole was one year older than Brian, and they loved hanging out together. Brian and Nicole were so cute together, and it was so fun to see my little brother growing up so fast.

Not long after the accident, Nicole and her family moved to another part of Utah. I can't imagine being just 10 years old and losing your best friend, then having to start over in a new place. Nicole reached out to me many years later, and shared the following visitation dream that she experienced almost two years after Brian's passing:

"After Brian passed away, I felt so empty. It was so hard for me to lose him, being so young and not really understanding what I was feeling. When we moved, I still carried that pain —for years. I did not make friends easily, and I was not very happy. I cried about losing Brian all the time. One weekend, in the summer of 1993, I had the most amazing dream. In this experience, I was still living in the house right across from yours, and I was looking at the front of your house, through the window. I was crying a lot, and felt so sad—I remember thinking that maybe if I looked hard enough and wished hard enough, Brian would come back!

In this dream, 'Somewhere Out There' came on the radio, and I began crying even harder. I felt someone touch my back and I turned around, and Brian was standing there. I hugged him and was telling him how excited I was, and that I could not wait to tell everyone. He told me that he could not stay with me and that he had just come to say goodbye. I hugged him and cried and told him that I missed him so much. He told me it was okay, that he was okay, and that I would be okay! For some reason it all made sense to me, and I woke up feeling *amazing*! I was crying, but it was a happy cry. I did not feel sad, or loss, or pain. I went downstairs to tell my parents what had happened, and as soon as I walked into the living room, 'Somewhere Out There' started playing on the radio, which my parents were listening to. Some people will say that this was just a dream, but to me, it was so much more. I needed that goodbye more than anything. It brought me peace! Now I can think of Brian and be happy, remembering all the amazing times we had; now I can think of Brian and smile!"

Indeed, this experience was much more than a dream—it was a visitation dream. Our regular dreams are generally fragmented distortions that run together and don't make much sense, whereas visitation dreams are undeniably memorable, *very* clear, and feel more real than waking life.

In September of 2007 I found out I was pregnant for the first time. It had taken longer to conceive than my husband and I had anticipated, and once it finally happened, we were over the moon. On the evening of this exciting day, I went to visit my mom so I could share the good news in person.

After our visit, on my drive home, I had my iPod set to shuffle, playing a compilation album that contained nearly two hundred songs. One of Brian's songs came on; it was "More Than Words," by Extreme. Brian loved this song, and although it is more of a romantic song, my family and I think of it as saying that he loves us and that we love him. I was really touched that this song had played on this special day, and I thought that perhaps it was Brian's way of saying "Congratulations." I feel that Brian was with my children in spirit before they came to Earth, and that he sent them here with all the love and care an uncle could possess.

I began crying happy tears, and called my mom to tell her about the sign I had just received. The song continued to play while my mom and I talked. Then the next song began, and it was another one of Brian's songs: "Kokomo," by the Beach Boys! This song came out a couple of years before the accident, and played often on the radio. Brian always perked up, more than he already naturally was, when he'd hear this song. Having both songs play back-to-back on this day in the car, was significant, since it was the very day that I found out I was pregnant. My mom and I both thought those were amazing signs from Brian, but then doubt kicked in and I started to wonder…was it just a coincidence, or were these really signs from Brian?

Even though my iPod was set to shuffle, both of those songs were on the album that was playing, so perhaps it was just a coincidence. Then my mom said, "Wouldn't it be amazing if 'Somewhere Out There' came on?" I replied, "Yes, that would be amazing, but I don't have that song in my collection." I was still driving, so we said goodbye.

Thoughts about signs and coincidences swirled around in my mind, so I decided to put it to the test, and I spoke out loud, saying, "Brian, I don't want to have any doubts. It can be so easy to think of these happenings as coincidences—please show me that they are not. *If* those songs were a sign, please play 'Somewhere Out There' next." I turned my iPod off and switched on the radio.

When I first tuned in, I knew that it wouldn't be possible for that song to play on the alternative station that it was set to, so I tuned in to a station that would be more likely to play that type of music. When I selected the station, there were ads running, so I just waited to see what would happen. As soon as the ads ended, my doubts were dispelled when "Somewhere Out There" began playing! I honestly could not believe my ears! It truly was a sign from

Brian, showing me that he was right there with me! This gave me the confirmation that I needed: the two previous songs were not coincidental.

I immediately called my mom and held my phone near the speaker. "Listen to this!" I exclaimed, as I increased the volume. I explained to her what had just happened, and we were both in awe. This experience taught me let go of doubt and that you don't have to wait for signs—you can *ask* for them!

We said goodbye and I said out loud, "Thank you Brian, thank you! And thank you for the opportunity that you gave me to be your big sister. You let me know what it was like to act as a mother figure, and I am so thankful for that. Thank you so much for giving me this sign today, and for clearing up any doubts I had."

Unfortunately, just a few days later, I miscarried. Not only was it difficult to lose a baby, but also to lose the future that my husband and I had envisioned—transitioning from a couple to a family. This new phase of life had just been stopped in its tracks. I felt so empty after this loss; however, on the bright side, I now knew that it was *possible* for me to get pregnant, which brought me the gift of hope. Envisioning my unborn child being with Brian until I can join them someday, brings me a lot of comfort.

In 2015, my grandad was diagnosed with a brain tumor, at the age of 91. He went in for surgery to have it removed, and although the tumor was successfully removed, he failed to wake up after the surgery. He was unresponsive, but was put on life support, in hopes that he would awaken. My cousin Kalie flew from Denver to Salt Lake City to visit our grandad in the hospital, and after sitting with him for a while, she decided to find something to watch on the television.

She flipped through the stations and landed on a channel where a choir was performing. As the song they were singing ended, the very next song was "Somewhere Out There." Kalie knew that "Somewhere Out There" was one of Brian's songs, and that it had been sung at his funeral. In the very moment that song began to play, she knew that Brian was right there in the hospital room, giving comfort to both her and to grandad. She was so glad that she made the effort to come see him, and that she was given this amazing sign. Flying to another state, turning on the TV, and hearing that song could not have had better timing. Sadly, after being on life support for some time, the decision was made to turn it off, and grandad passed away. Kalie's experience has given us reassurance, knowing that Brian and grandad are now together.

During the time my grandad was on life support, my mom had an appointment to see her primary care doctor, whose office is in the same hospital. Even though my parents are divorced, my grandad was her father-in-law for 16 years, and she thought it would be nice to check in on him since she was already there.

As she walked into the hospital lobby, the pianist was playing "Somewhere Out There." I am so thankful to Brian for letting us know he is with us still, and that he and my grandad are together. On Valentine's Day the next year, in 2016, right as my mom walked into the senior center which she frequently visits, the pianist was playing "Somewhere Out There," and she considered it a Valentine's gift from Brian.

"MORE THAN WORDS"

"More Than Words" by Extreme came out in March of 1991, seven months prior to the accident. It was a very popular song and played on the radio often. Brian loved it, and he would sing along to it every time it came on in the car, or the radio at home. So now, whenever my family and I hear it, we remember how he would sing along and we think of it as a reciprocal saying: we love Brian "more than words" can say, and he feels the same towards us.

When my son was just a toddler, in 2010, he and I were hanging out at home, and I was thinking about Brian and missing him. With sincere longing, I said out loud, "I miss you, Bri." The next day when my son and I were hanging out, I turned on the radio, which was set to soft classics. "More Than Words" came on shortly after I turned on the radio, and two songs later, "Kokomo" played. I just knew that these songs were a hello from Brian. I listen to that station all the time and have never heard either of those songs play. To hear them both so close together, when just the day before I had spoken out loud and told Brian that I missed him, showed me that he is there when I think of him—just as all our loved ones are.

On what would have been Brian's 29th birthday in June of 2011, I watched some old family videos so that I could feel close and connected with him. Afterwards, I turned on some music from my husband's iPod as I prepared dinner. There are thousands of songs in his collection, and I set it to shuffle. As I was cooking, "More Than Words" came on. In my husband's entire collection, he only has two songs that were Brian's favorites. With the thousands of songs that could have played on Brian's birthday, it was this one! I thought it was so special that he gave me a sign to say hello, on this special day, after I'd just finished watching him on video—the timing was impeccable.

On Brian's birthday in 2014, my dad went out for a drive. He was thinking about Brian and missing him terribly. He turned on the radio and flipped through the stations to find a song he liked. Nothing caught his fancy, so he just left it on a random station, and the next song that played was "More Than Words." My dad had not heard that song in years, and we agree that it is no coincidence that it played right on Brian's birthday, just as my dad was reflecting about him.

Back when my grandad was on life support in late 2015, he was staying at the University of Utah hospital, which is right next to Primary Children's Hospital, where Brian passed away. My dad was on his way to go see Grandad, but just as he was driving past Primary Children's Hospital, "More Than Words" began playing over the radio. The last time he had heard that song was on Brian's birthday a year earlier. Additionally, this happened just a few days before the anniversary of the accident.

One day in 2015, my mom came over to my house for a visit. The commotion in the house was loud, as my kids, ages four and six, were excited to be with grandma and were running around. The radio was softly playing in the background, but there was so much noise that I had forgotten the radio was even on. When it came time for my mom to leave, we said our goodbyes and I closed the front door. The kids calmed down as I looked out the window at my mom pulling out of the driveway. In this moment I could finally hear the radio, and "More Than Words" was playing as I watched my mom leave. I took this as a sign that Brian had been there visiting, too.

Every day, my sister Kristin turns the radio on *before* she leaves her house, as she likes her dog to have something to listen to. One morning in 2017, she felt prompted to turn it on right *after* she woke up, which was not her normal routine. She followed the nudge she was receiving, and just as she turned the radio on, "More Than Words" started playing. Something prompted her to turn the radio on at that time, and she knew that something was Brian, just saying hello. If she hadn't been present enough to tune in to that little prodding, she would have missed the opportunity to receive that sign.

In the summer of 2018, my kids and I hopped into the car after leaving the doctor's office for their annual checkups. I switched the stereo from my iPod to the radio, intentionally hoping to hear one of Brian's songs. The very next song that played on the radio was "More Than Words!" I couldn't believe it, and I told my kids that I had been hoping for one of Brian's songs. Just then, I realized that the very next day was Brian's birthday! Out of all the songs, and all the days that I could have heard that song, there it was, right at that time.

The very next summer, in 2019, the same thing happened, but my kids and I were at the grocery store. I knew that the next day was Brian's birthday, so I told my kids, "Hey guys, remember what happened last year, the day before Brian's birthday? Since his birthday is tomorrow, I am expecting a sign from him soon." Just as we got into the car, "More Than Words" began to play on the radio. The last time I heard that song was exactly one year earlier, and both times were the day before Brian's birthday.

Later in 2019, I had a very difficult and stressful decision to make, regarding my health. I went to pick up my kids at the school, and to see my sister Kristin who teaches there. I told her that I was feeling at peace after making my decision, and I knew that Brian had given me guidance. My kids and I said goodbye to Kristin and went on our way. As we were pulling out of the school parking lot, my son pointed to a heart-shaped cloud and said, "I bet that heart cloud is from Brian!" I replied, "You are right!" I quickly snapped a picture of the cloud, and within seconds, my aunt Cobie messaged me, saying that she had just heard "More Than Words" on the radio.

On the 29th anniversary of the accident in 2020, my mom went to a restaurant for lunch. As she sat and looked over the menu, she was thinking about how much she missed Brian, and just then, "More Than Words" began playing. She knew it was a sign that Brian was also thinking of her.

In May of 2021, I called my dad, and we were talking about Brian's songs. He was saying that he'd only heard "More Than Words" twice since Brian's passing, but they were both at significant times. The very next morning, my dad went outside to do some yardwork, and as he put on his headphones, the very first song that came on was "More Than Words." Like I said, since Brian's passing in 1991, he has only heard that song *twice*. It was amazing that this third time was just the day after we had been discussing it. That tells me that Brian is close and he is still here, just in a different form.

"FAITH"

Another song that Brian loved was "Faith" by George Michael, and my family and I consider it one of "Brian's songs" because he and Erika used to lip-synch and play air guitar to it in front of the TV as they recorded themselves. Images of him strumming his imaginary guitar as he giggled, come rushing back to our memories whenever we hear it, always causing a smile to sweep across our faces.

In February of 2018 when my son was nine years old, he became very ill, and had been sick for longer than I felt was normal. I had spoken with the nurse at his pediatrician's office, who told me that this sickness was going around, and that it should improve soon. One evening, his fever finally broke and he began to show a little bit of improvement. I expected that he'd be on the road to recovery, and I looked forward to him getting back to his usual self. However, the next morning, his fever returned, along with some new symptoms that began to water the worry that was now growing in my mind.

I immediately made an appointment with his pediatrician, and he was able to see us that morning. On our way there, the radio played in the background, but it hadn't caught my attention until I suddenly realized that "Faith" by George Michael was playing. I thought about how I hadn't heard that song in a while, and then I smiled when it dawned on me that this was one of Brian's songs. I felt he was sending me a message, as not only was it one of his songs, but the title, "Faith," was speaking to me, reminding me to trust that everything would turn out okay. A few weeks prior, I had asked Brian for a sign, and now… here it was!

The pediatrician examined my son and diagnosed him with Periorbital Cellulitis, and we were immediately sent to the hospital. My husband met us there, and after some scans, it was discovered that the cellulitis was very close to reaching his brain. The doctor whose care he was now under described this bacterium as "strong enough to walk through walls." My son was admitted right away and was put on IV antibiotics, in hopes that they would curtail the need for a risky surgery. As all of this was happening, my mind reverted to the sign I received earlier, and I remembered to have faith. By this time, my husband had left to care for our daughter. I stayed by my son's side, until a nurse informed me that I had a visitor. I was confused, because nobody other than my husband was aware of this situation yet. How was it possible that I would have a visitor?

I curiously went into the hallway and was met by a stranger, followed by the warmest hug that I have ever received. This was another mom who had been in a similar situation—her name was Sarah. She explained that her son is a patient of the same doctor that my son was now seeing. She and her son had just been in for a checkup, and the doctor mentioned that there was a little boy in the hospital who was diagnosed with what her son had just recovered from. After hearing this, she rushed over to offer me comfort—mother to mother. She wholeheartedly reassured me that the doctor was truly the best, and not to worry. This reaffirmed to me to have faith—and I did. Thankfully, the antibiotics were successful in fighting my son's infection, and he didn't need to undergo the surgery; however, in Sarah's son's case, he developed an even more serious condition (necrotizing fasciitis), on top of the cellulitis. Her son was allergic to the first three antibiotics that were administered to him, which necessitated two surgeries to clear the infection. This situation happened a little over a month earlier, right on New Year's Eve, when her son was only four years old.

Miraculously, my son made a full recovery. I am so grateful for the signs I get from Brian, especially at times when I really need them. I will be forever grateful to the other mom, Sarah, who came to reinforce Brian's message to have faith, and for acting as an earth angel to bring me the comfort that I desperately needed at that time. I know that Brian played a part in sending her to me.

In one of my son's follow-up appointments, his doctor shared some great advice with us. He said, "You might be paranoid about germs after all of this, but don't be. Live life. Keep doing the things that you want to do, and go to the places that you want to go. People get sick when they touch their eyes, nose, or mouth. Just wash your hands often and keep them off your face. But remember —live life." I loved this advice so much that I had a bracelet made with the words "Live Life" engraved on it. I love wearing it as a reminder to do just that.

In April of 2018, before I went to bed, I asked Brian to give me a sign soon. The next afternoon, I hopped into my car, and I caught the last few seconds of "Faith" on the radio. Because I had asked Brian for a sign, I knew that it was from him.

"KOKOMO"

"Kokomo" by The Beach Boys was one of Brian's favorite songs. He would just light up whenever it would play on the radio, which was often, because it released only a couple of years before the accident. Whenever I hear it, I picture Brian on the beach, doing one of his favorite things—chasing seagulls.

On Brian's birthday in 2021, my dad and I were talking about the signs that we've received from Brian over the years. I reminded him that "Kokomo" was one of Brian's songs. My dad didn't realize this, since that song was released after my parents' divorce, and he must not have been there when Brian listened to it.

The very next evening, my dad got into bed and asked his smart speaker to play songs by The Eagles. Three Eagles songs proceeded to play, but the fourth song that played was "Kokomo," which is by The Beach Boys, not The Eagles. My dad was amazed, and of course, I was too when he shared this experience with me. If we hadn't had the discussion the day before about "Kokomo," he wouldn't have ever known that it was one of Brian's songs. Brian is right there listening, and he figures out ways to grab our attention.

Each year, as the air begins to crisp and the leaves begin to change color, a bit of melancholy sweeps over my family and me, knowing that the anniversary of the accident is approaching. In October of 2022, sadness about the upcoming anniversary had crept in. I was especially missing Brian, more than usual, and I was yearning for a sign from him. So, I asked him if he would give me, or a family member, a sign within the next couple of days.

The next morning, which marked *exactly* 30 years since the accident, my Aunt Cobie sent me a text saying that she had heard "Faith" on the radio. Later that afternoon, I was listening to a podcast in my car, and remembered that I needed to make it possible for Brian to come through. So, I switched on the radio and said out loud, "Okay Bri, play one of your songs," and then immediately after my request, "Kokomo" came on!

"SEE YOU AGAIN"

"See You Again" by Wiz Khalifa, featuring Charlie Puth, is a more recent song that my family and I now consider to be one of "Brian's songs" for this modern era. I think it's so neat that Brian has chosen an updated song as one of his signs.

In October of 2019, just two days before the anniversary of the accident, I went to lunch with a good friend. I was emotional as I told her the anniversary was soon approaching, and I said to her, "This Friday, it will have been 28 years since I've seen my brother… it's been such a long time without him." I was expecting a sign from Brian soon, because of the pending anniversary. After lunch, as I got into my car, the song "See You Again" came on the radio. Although, at the time, this was not one of Brian's songs, I was shocked by the lyrics, because they were repeating almost the exact words that I had just said to my friend. On top of that, some other parts of the lyrics were almost identical to what's written on Brian's headstone—I felt strongly that this song was a sign from Brian. I told my family about what happened, and we all agreed that is one of Brian's "new" songs.

On my mom's birthday in 2020, she went up to the cemetery to spend some time at Brian's graveside. The radio was playing, and she asked Brian to play one of his songs. Her solicitation was made out loud, but even if she had just asked in her mind, her request would have been received. Immediately, "See You Again" started playing. The drive to the cemetery from my mom's house is only a couple of minutes away. My mom was shocked at how quickly Brian responded with a sign, and that she was able to receive a sign in that little window of time, since the drive was so short.

In June of 2020, on Brian's birthday, I had the radio on all day, hoping to hear one of his songs. By the end of the day, I was discouraged that I hadn't heard any of them. I was thinking about Brian just before I turned the radio off, and "See You Again" came on at that moment. I was amazed that Brian gave me a song at the last possible moment that he could have on this special date— almost as if he was saving it as a little treat before I went to bed. The first time I heard that song was that same year, in October, the day before the anniversary of the accident. Although it has been a long time, I know that I will see you again, Brian.

"PIECE OF MY HEART"

Every time my dad goes to visit Brian's graveside, he repeats a lullaby that reads: "Sleep my child, sleep my son, sleep little piece of my heart," which he recites in Spanish.

Exactly 30 years after Brian's passing, on October 5th, 2021, my dad got up early to visit Brian at his resting place, which he does on this date every year. After a quick stop at the grocery store to purchase a dozen roses, my dad was on his way. In the back of his mind, he hoped that maybe Brian would send him a sign, either a song or message of some kind. My dad thought, "It's been mostly music in the past, but this time, any legitimate contact, or message, will finally remove any doubt that past messages might have been simply a series of amazing coincidences."

Although he hoped for a sign that day, he wasn't holding any high expectations. He didn't want to make something out of nothing or misinterpret anything as a coincidence. He simply wanted to allow whatever might come his way and let the day unfold.

On his way to the cemetery, my dad recited the lullaby in Spanish. Just as he finished, he pulled into the parking lot, and as he was about to open the car door, displayed on his stereo screen was the last line of the lullaby he had just recited, "Piece of my Heart!" He had to do a double take, as he could hardly believe his eyes! Although "Piece of my Heart," by Janis Joplin, is not one of Brian's songs, the fact that the title displayed at that exact moment, was incredible, and my dad took it as a very clear sign from Brian, which let him know that Brian was right beside him.

CHRISTMAS SONGS

Growing up, our family had a Christmas album that was a compilation of various artists. We would repeatedly play it every Christmas season during our childhood. Brian specifically loved two of the songs on that album: the version of "Winter Wonderland" sung by Dolly Parton, and "Feliz Navidad" by José Feliciano. I choreographed a dance to "Winter Wonderland" for my siblings and I to perform one year for a Christmas family talent show, and I once recorded Kristin and Brian performing the dance together in our living room. Whenever any of my family members and I hear it, we think of Brian and these performances.

Brian would lip-synch to "Feliz Navidad" in front of the TV, while watching himself as he recorded his performance. He was such a little character, and hearing this song always makes me picture him rapidly shrugging his shoulders up and down as he mouthed the lyrics, trying his very best not to burst out laughing.

On Christmas Eve of 2007, I put together a DVD of some old family videos to give my family. I love to keep Brian in our memories by giving gifts that remind us of him. The DVD included the recordings of the performances I just mentioned.

I woke up around 7:30 am on Christmas morning, and laid in bed as I looked out the window into the snow globe-inspired scene. I laid there for an hour, listening to the Christmas music that was softly playing on the radio that I had left on all night. "Winter Wonderland" started playing, and in that moment, the sun shined so brightly that it literally lit up the room. It was so calm, peaceful, and beautiful, and as I looked out the window I could see the rays of the sun hitting the freshly fallen snow, looking like the world had just been sprinkled with glittering fairy dust. Shortly after that, "Feliz Navidad" began playing, just as I was about to hop out of bed, and I knew that this was Brian's way of wishing me a "Merry Christmas." The light and the music were as if he was floating above me, orchestrating the whole thing, like a conductor.

Later that day when my family gathered, I gave them each a copy of the DVD, and we all sat down and watched it together. As we watched, I realized how significant that morning was, because both songs that played while lying in bed were the same songs that Brian performed on the DVD that I had made just the night before, and I knew that my experience that morning was Brian's gift to me.

HOLD ON TO DEAR LIFE

The "Hold on to Dear Life" campaign began in 1990, in the state of Utah. It was a public service campaign sponsored by Primary Children's Hospital, and its focus was on seatbelt use and car seat safety. Even though most of us were not wearing our seatbelts on the day of the accident, we are all very cognizant about wearing them now. Not long after our car accident, my parents were contacted by the campaign leaders to ask for permission to feature Brian's picture in one of the commercials; my parents were more than happy to oblige.

Each "Hold on to Dear Life" advertisement played the same jingle throughout the entirety of every commercial. It was very poignant, and hearing it makes me tear up, even to this day. The lyrics are:

> *"Hold on to Dear Life,*
> *And every precious smile.*
> *We're only here together,*
> *For just a little while...*
> *Hold on to dear life."*

On the morning of what would have been Brian's 30th birthday in 2012, my mom and I spoke on the phone about him, and then together, we both asked Brian for a sign. After we got off the phone, my mom was watching TV, and a "Hold on to Dear Life" commercial began playing. There were many commercials within the campaign, but the one that came on this day was the one that featured Brian's picture! In this commercial, Brian's picture is the very first photo to appear, and is followed by pictures of several other children who also lost their lives due to not being properly restrained. When the commercial began playing, my mom saw this image spread across her television screen...

Anytime you'd watch TV in the early 90s, it was standard to see one of the "Hold on to Dear Life" commercials, but by the mid-

2000s, the commercials didn't run nearly as frequently. In fact, it was extremely rare to catch one of them by this time.

It wasn't magic that my mom "happened" to see Brian's picture appear across the screen on her TV, right on Brian's birthday—it was a sign from Brian. She was so grateful to him for sharing this gift with her on his birthday.

Three years later, on October 5th, 2015 (the anniversary date of Brian's passing), my mom was watching the local evening news, and to her surprise, they were doing a story about the 25th Anniversary of the "Hold on to Dear Life" campaign. The news anchors shared one of the commercials from the campaign, and the one they shared was Brian's! Once again, my mom saw Brian's picture spread across her screen. It was so nice for my mom to receive another magical gift from Brian, especially on this significant date.

13

SPRINKLING OF SIGNS

When my family and I receive signs from Brian, it's generally on significant dates like birthdays and anniversaries, but not always. Sometimes the signs are just sprinkled into random, regular days, and sometimes they've even been lifesaving.

The night my mom chose Brian's headstone, she returned home with a very heavy heart. This was in the early spring of 1992, after all the snow from winter had melted—approximately six months after Brian's death. She was desperately missing her son, and knelt to pray.

As she closed her eyes, she saw a vision of Brian in what she describes as her "mind's eye." It appeared to be either dusk or dawn, because he was silhouetted as he walked along the edge of a stream, kicking rocks. She kept asking him to turn around so that she could see his sweet face, but he just kept kicking rocks, and seemed to be at peace. She said it was like watching a movie, so she just stayed down on her knees and watched him for a long time. At one point, she opened her eyes for a few seconds, but hoped the movie in her mind wouldn't end. To her delight, upon closing her eyes again, Brian was still there. This experience was so healing for my mom, and she longed to have another one. Little did she know, there were many more signs from Brian to come.

In 1994, my mom was repainting the inside of her home, and after she finished, she pulled the tape off the sides of an exposed outlet in her bathroom. She was about to put a screwdriver into the outlet because a wire looked out of place. Just as she went to touch one of the wires with her screwdriver, she heard a very loud and startling noise that stopped her from what she was about to do. The noise came from her bedroom, and she knew that something very heavy had fallen. She raced to see what had fallen, as the screwdriver dropped from her hands.

She found that the two heavy wooden table leaves that belonged to our dining room table were lying flat on the floor. The leaves had been stored in her closet and only saw the light of day during the holidays. The leaves had been placed upright and were positioned to lean diagonally from the floor to the closet wall, to keep them from tipping over. To have fallen, they would have needed to be pushed from the end where they rested against the wall. My mom is convinced that the only thing that could have made them fall—was Brian. This is a great example of how spirit beings can physically touch or move an object.

In February of 2013, just a random day, I was thinking about Brian and missing him a lot. I had the easy listening radio station on as I was making lunch, and I realized that "I'll Be There," by the Jackson Five was playing. Brian *loved* Michael Jackson, and hearing Michael Jackson's voice made me miss and think of Brian even more. Starting at the age of just two years old, Brian confiscated the family turkey baster, turning it into a makeshift microphone. I can still picture him swiftly tapping one heel up and down, while lip-synching to Michael Jackson's "Beat-It," "Billie Jean," and "Thriller." Brian would do the moonwalk the best he could on the shag carpet in the living room, adding in a spin here and there, as he tried not to topple over. My sisters and I would repeatedly rewind the songs for him, day in and day out, until he turned four and found his new obsession with the New Kids on the Block. Whenever my family and I hear any of those Michael Jackson songs, we remember Brian with his "microphone," and we smile.

When "I'll Be There" was playing, I realized that even though this song wasn't one of his favorites, the artist was, and the lyrics were speaking to me, as if Brian was sending me a message. I could feel his strong presence, and I suddenly felt a *very* warm sensation inside my heart. I am so grateful that Brian let me know that if I just call his name, he'll be there.

It is the same for us all: when you need your loved one, just call their name.

As soon as that song ended, the next song began playing as I continued making lunch. I didn't pay much attention, as I was thinking about what had just happened, but once I turned my focus to the music, I realized it was the song "God Bless the U.S.A.," by Lee Greenwood, which Brian had *loved* to sing. I called my mom to tell her about these signs, and she thought it was so neat that Brian had given me a message through the lyrics of the Jackson Five song, and she also remembered that Brian loved singing "God Bless the U.S.A," which neither of us had heard in at least a decade! We both reminisced about how cute it was when Brian would parade around the house singing that song as loudly as he could.

Another sign related to Michael Jackson happened in the summer of 2024. I wanted to connect with Brian, so I thought about the song that most reminds me of him, which is "Billie Jean," and I asked him for that. I figured that I'd hear the song as I went about my day, or that maybe I'd overhear someone mention it. However, I received my sign in a way that I never expected.

I enjoy reading celebrity news magazines, and the next day I was looking through the latest issue while my husband drove us to the grocery store. As I flipped through the pages, I suddenly froze —I happened to stop on a page that had a story about a famous tennis player named Billie Jean King. I had never heard of this woman, but there was my sign—not as a song, but in print! I thought this was such a unique way for him to send me this sign—I love it!

Not long after this experience, I decided to ask Brian for one of his songs, "More Than Words." I was driving and thought that maybe I'd hear it in the car, but I didn't. When I arrived home, I checked my social media and came across a post by a friend. She had shared a picture of herself and her new boyfriend, with text written across their photo—wishing her new love a happy birthday and calling him a miracle in her life. Directly below that, standing on its own, were the words "More than words."

I was awestruck to receive another sign that I'd expected to hear as a song, but instead received in print.

14

SPECIFIC SIGNS

When asking for signs, it helps to be specific, just like the sign I just shared about "Billie Jean." If you just ask for a "sign," it can be easily missed because you don't know what type of sign to look for. When you're specific about what you want, your loved one knows exactly what to deliver and you know exactly what to expect. Below are some examples of times that my family and I have asked for very specific signs, and Brian has delivered.

On the last day of May, in 2021, my husband and I took our kids to the local amusement park. My daughter, who was 10 years old, was riding the sky lift with me. As it carried us from one side of the park to the other, I took advantage of the time to reminisce with her about the signs that Brian has sent over the years. I have shared many of these signs with my kids, and they've witnessed some of them happening, but I wanted her to know that she can ask her Uncle Brian for signs herself.

I reminded her that Brian is her angel uncle who is watching over all of us. I said to her, "Let's just try asking Brian for a sign, and see what happens." I told her that we could ask for anything, whether it be a certain type of bird, a butterfly, a coin, feather, or even a frog—whatever she wanted. She replied with, "Let's ask Brian to bring us Finn the cat!"

I had *no* idea who Finn the cat was, so when I asked her, she explained that Finn is an orange and white tabby that came into our yard, *once*, about a year ago. I responded by saying, "That's a pretty specific sign to ask for, and might be difficult for him to deliver. Why don't we just ask Brian for an orange tabby?"

Because signs are not always literal and can be received in many, often unexpected ways, such as appearing on a screen (television, movie, or social media feed), or in print (books, license plates, street signs, billboards, receipts, bumper stickers), I explained to her that our sign could be anywhere, and said, "Let's just be aware and keep our eyes open for an orange tabby." She agreed, and we asked Brian to fulfill this request within the next two days.

Shortly after arriving home, I went into the backyard to throw away some trash. Right after I tossed the trash bag into the garbage can, I heard a distinct "meow," and looked over to see an orange tabby cat sitting on our back porch steps! I immediately rushed inside, through the garage door, and excitedly told my daughter that Brian had given us our sign. Together, we ran outside, and as we walked towards the steps where the cat was still sitting, she cried, "Mom, that's Finn! Remember? I asked for Finn! You said not to get that specific, but Brian did it! He sent Finn to us!" I approached the cat, and as I turned the tag on its collar over, I was stunned, yet delighted, to see that it read "Finn." We were both completely in awe to have received this sign from Brian, and especially to have received it *only* within an hour of asking. Brian confirmed to us that we can, indeed, be specific when we ask for signs. I sensed an "I'll show you!" from Brian, and boy, did he ever show us! My daughter and I both looked up and said, "Thank you, Brian!"

Because our loved ones on the other side exist as a different form of energy, they can give us signs through animals. They can choose to use their energy to either influence an animal's actions, or they can enter the animal. By doing this, it allows them to physically interact with this world.

In July of 2021, my sister Erika was thinking about hummingbirds, and how they are commonly interpreted as a sign from loved ones. Hummingbirds are associated with the spirit world in many cultures, particularly with Native Americans, and are interpreted as a message that your loved one is watching over you and sending love. She had never received any signs with birds, so this inspired her to ask Brian for a hummingbird. She then went outside, where her husband was doing some yard work. He suddenly called over to her, "Look, honey! There's a hummingbird sitting on your roses!"

Erika was shocked, and recalls, "We watched it for a while, and it just sat on one of my roses and stared at us. I've never seen a hummingbird near my roses, and I've also never seen one sit still like that. I felt like there was no doubt that it was Brian. Especially because I had just asked him for that!" The sequence of this is what made it an especially significant sign. Thinking about hummingbirds as a sign, asking for one, and then seeing one, all within a couple of minutes, was truly a "wow moment" for her!

One day I was thinking about the things that Brian liked, and thought it would be fun to ask him for something other than music, so I thought about what he loved and decided upon Teenage Mutant Ninja Turtles. This was August of 2021, and I hadn't heard of, or seen, any of them since around the time of the accident, which was 30 years ago at that time. So I asked, "Brian, show me a Teenage Mutant Ninja Turtle sometime soon."

The next evening, I was getting ready for bed and had left the TV on the main menu of Netflix, intending to put something on once I got into bed. The TV sat in silence, displaying the main menu as I brushed my teeth and enjoyed the quiet stillness. Suddenly, the TV began playing, and all I could hear was someone repeating the words, "Teenage Mutant Ninja Turtles." I looked at the TV to discover that it was a trailer for a show that was all about their history and how they came to be. I was so amazed that I had received my sign so quickly, and I went to bed with a big smile on my face.

A couple days later, I went into a local bakery, and just as I walked in, there was a woman wearing a Teenage Mutant Ninja Turtles T-shirt. Since when do you see a middle-aged woman wearing a T-shirt like that? Once again, I was amazed.

In 2023, my mom decided to ask Brian for flocks of birds as a sign, and she has since witnessed huge flocks, multiple times. For example, on Christmas Day that year, a flock flew in synchronicity right over her car as she was leaving my sister's house, and another flock swooped directly over her car right on the anniversary date of the accident. Each time she has seen them, she is amazed. However, I have had a difficult time accepting that it's really a sign, because part of me reasons that maybe it's simply a flock of birds. But, over time, I have come to realize that flocks of birds can be a sign.

Birds are widely considered signs from loved ones, as throughout the Bible, God sends birds as messengers. Birds also represent freedom, love, and peace. It is a commonly held belief that birds are powerful symbols, offering comfort and meaning after the loss of a loved one. Any bird will do, but the most common birds associated with signs are hummingbirds, cardinals, doves, robins, and blue jays. Just as I've talked about getting specific, you can ask your loved one for whatever sign you'd like. So, I decided to see for myself, and asked Brian for a flock of birds. I told him that if he could send me one on this day, I would accept that flocks of birds can be a sign. I only left the house that day for a short trip to the grocery store, and I didn't see any flocks of birds; however, that afternoon while I was on social media, I scrolled down the page and came upon a photo of a huge flock of birds. The caption of "Murmuration" was listed just below the photo. Murmuration is when a large group of birds fly together in intricately coordinated patterns and change direction together—a flock!

It was amazing to see a picture of a flock, and the description of a flock, on the *very* day that I had asked Brian to show me that flocks of birds are really a sign. Again, I was wowed, and I appreciated that Brian verified this sign for me.

On Christmas Eve in 2023, I asked Brian if he would give me a sign on Christmas. I asked to see another Teenage Mutant Ninja Turtle. I wasn't sure how that would be possible, since we were staying home all day for Christmas. Because of that, I said that any other sign he's sent in the past would work as an alternative. After the festivities were over, I was putting away decorations, and as I went to place a silver star in the storage box, I thought it was too pretty to be tucked away all year. So, I looked for a place to display it, and was drawn to my office bookcase.

As I was placing the star, I arranged it next to some things that are important to me: a picture of Brian, the vase that holds the rods that were once in my legs, and Brian's Ninja Turtle that I had chosen from his box of things after his room had been cleared out. Suddenly, it dawned on me that I was touching Brian's Ninja Turtle —and there was my sign! When I asked for the sign, I wanted to allow it to happen naturally, without seeking it out; therefore, it was tucked so far back in my mind, that I didn't realize I had been given what I had asked for until the moment I was touching it. I know that Brian guided me to find a new home for the star, which brought me straight to his Ninja Turtle. I looked up and thanked Brian for that amazing Christmas gift.

15

COINS

Coins are another common sign that loved ones can send. Throughout history and in many cultures, coins have been used in funeral rituals to honor the departed. Originating in Greek culture, coins would be placed in the mouth, or near the body, to prepare the deceased for burial. It served as the fare they believed was required to pass between the world of the living and the world of the dead. The Romans also adopted this practice, especially for the graves of fallen soldiers, symbolizing payment for the soldier's journey to the afterlife. This ritual spread throughout the empire.

In modern times, leaving coins on the graves of military personnel in the U.S. and Canada is a common ritual, to "pay one's respects," which displays honor to the departed, and is a way to let family members know that someone has visited. Today, coins are believed to be a sign from departed loved ones, as they can be easily moved by spiritual beings, and represent a token of love. Typically, the coins sit in our path, and are not hard to miss. They can be any type of coin, and can even be items that look like coins.

My sister Kristin has had several experiences with coins. She is a first-grade teacher, and in 2018, she had just been through a breakup and was feeling disheartened and alone. Just as she was feeling overwhelmed by all her emotions, one of her students randomly handed her a penny. Kristin smiled and felt it was a sign from Brian, letting her know that she is *never* alone. In 2020, she was feeling overburdened with life, and went out to her yard to do some gardening. As she moved the earth around, there in the dirt sat a shiny penny—just waiting to be noticed. Again, she smiled and knew it was Brian's way of letting her know that he was right by her side.

Then in 2023, Kristin and her daughter Emma were walking out of a store parking lot towards their car, and a penny rolled right up to them. Nobody else was around, and as Emma picked it up, Kristin told her, "It's yours." Emma had been going through a difficult time, and Kristin wanted her to cheer up. However, Kristin was hoping to get one as well, and as they took just a few more steps, there sat one more perfect penny at her feet—waiting just for her.

One afternoon in 2021, while my kids were having their tennis lesson, I sat on the grass reflecting on the signs we've received from Brian over the years, particularly the signs with coins. I thought about the coins that Kristin has received, and a time when Erika and I went out to dinner together and a shiny new penny sat directly in our path as we were leaving the restaurant. When this happened, we felt as if Brian had joined us for dinner that night.

As soon as my kids' tennis lesson ended, we walked to the car, and right before I opened the car door for my daughter, she bent down and picked up what looked like a penny, sitting right in her path. She handed it to me, and I was elated to see that it was a coin-shaped copper pendant with the word LOVE imprinted on it. This was most definitely a token of love. I knew it was from Brian, and I was amazed at how this played out, because when I initially parked the car, for some reason I decided to move my car to the next spot over. If I hadn't have done that, the pendant wouldn't have been in her path, and she would have missed it.

Sometimes it's just mind-boggling how these things happen.

This experience caused me to reflect on Erika's sign with the hummingbirds: thinking about them, asking for one, and then seeing one within a minute. Similarly, in this experience, I had just been reminiscing about our experiences with coins, and within a couple of minutes, one appeared directly in my daughter's path. I still have this pendant, and have put it on a chain to wear; I always think of Brain when it is close to my heart.

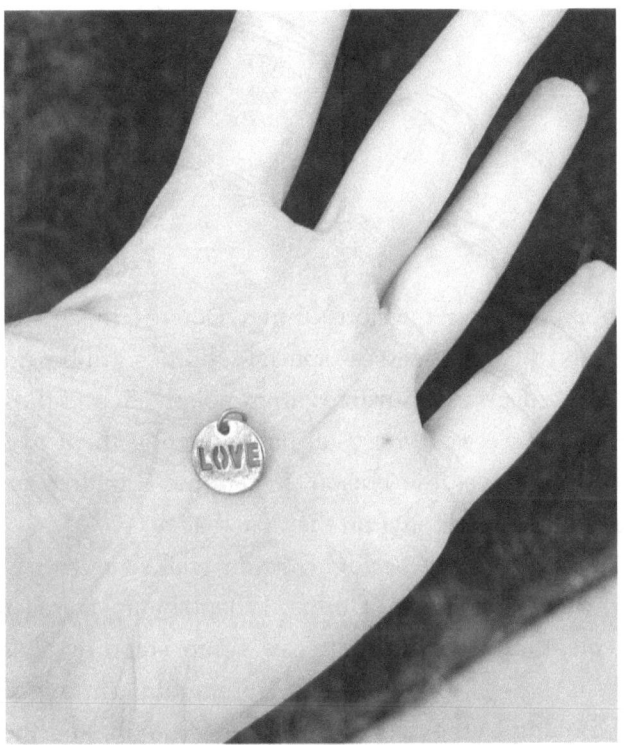

16

PREMONITIONS

Premonitions are a mysterious thing. Does it mean the person experiencing them possesses special abilities, unbeknownst to them? Does it mean that our lives are preplanned, and these people have somehow accessed a crystal ball, allowing them to peer into the future? Whatever the reason, it gets me thinking about how there is so much more going on than we realize.

Two days before the accident, Brian walked over to visit our lovely neighbor and friend, Donna. When she answered the door, she was pleasantly surprised to see Brian standing there. Brian asked, "What smells so good?" and Donna told him that she had a meatloaf cooking in the oven. She invited Brian in, and they talked for a few minutes. She recalled that he looked *so* bright, clean, and glowing. His glow caught her attention so much that she even asked, "Brian, did you just have a bath?" Brian told her that he hadn't, but as he turned to leave, his glow was even more pronounced. As she watched him walk away, she was puzzled as to why he seemed so bright.

Not long after the accident, Donna spoke with my mom, relaying that when she had heard of Brian's passing, she immediately reflected on that day when Brian had stopped by, and how undeniably distinct the luminosity around him was.

Upon reflection, Donna realized that the radiance that surrounded Brian that day must have meant that he was going to be called back to Heaven soon. This type of glow that surrounds a person prior to death is a phenomenon that can happen before someone passes—it's like the person who is going to pass already has one foot in Heaven's door.

Donna recalled, "I have never seen anyone look so beautiful; he had such a beautiful glow all around him. I feel so blessed to have witnessed the lovely gift of seeing precious Brian before he went to be with his Father in Heaven. It will be a memory I will treasure forever."

A night or two before the accident, one of Brian's best friends, Wynn, had a nightmare in which he was watching our car from behind, as if he were floating. He saw our car swerve one way, then the other, then it flipped, which was identical to what happened in the accident. Wynn said, "As the car began to roll, I woke up." The next morning, he was extremely bothered by the nightmare, and didn't know what to think about it.

Wynn shared, "On Monday, just after we were dropped off at school, my sister ran up to me and asked if I had heard that Brian had died. I was in shock. I was too young to process everything, as it was my first experience of losing someone close to me. My mom picked me up early from school, and when she told me that a car accident is what had killed Brian, I lost it and felt guilty, like I could have done something to prevent it. Thankfully, my mom really helped guide me through my emotions. Throughout the years, I've had weird instances where my dreams were prophetic, but nothing as specific as this event."

Both Donna's and Wynn's premonitions bring me comfort in knowing that it was Brian's time. I can see how the glow that Donna witnessed, could represent that Brian was being called back home. And I feel that because Wynn's dream depicted exactly what happened, perhaps Brian's departure was destined to happen the way that it did. These examples cause me to consider that maybe everything is as it should be, even when those things are difficult, and that what happens in this life is by design and there is a larger purpose at play.

17

LUCY IN THE SKY WITH BRIAN

On the morning of December 2nd, 2020, I was driving my kids to their elementary school on what seemed like an ordinary day. I had no idea everything that followed would reshape me in ways I never could have imagined. I noticed a woman walking her dog along the side of the road, and before I could blink, we felt and heard a loud thump—a sound I couldn't forget if I tried.

In that moment, my heart dropped—one of my worst nightmares had just occurred. I immediately pulled over and told my kids to stay in the car. I ran to the woman and her dog—while my thoughts and heart raced swiftly ahead of me. She was okay, but her little dog was badly injured. While she ran to get her parents, who lived nearby, I stayed with the dog—a sweet, short-haired dachshund with a glossy, dark-brown coat. During this time, I looked into the dog's eyes, praying she would survive, while offering my most sincere apologies.

When the woman returned with her father, I braced myself for anger. Blame. Harsh words. But instead, her father looked at me with compassion and said two words: "Thank you." The woman echoed his kindness, saying "Things happen; thank you for staying with her." As they drove away, I stood there shaking—overwhelmed not only by the trauma of what had just taken place, but by the unexpected grace they had just shown me.

My legs shook like jelly as I walked back to my car where my kids patiently waited. I made sure they were feeling alright before dropping them off at school. Luckily, they were unscathed; however, I was not—I went home sobbing, trembling, and in shock.

In the coming days, I felt extremely unsettled. The accident kept replaying in my mind, and I was riddled with grief. I *needed* to know: did the dog survive? How was the woman coping? I searched for their home carrying flowers and a sympathy card to express how sorry I was. But, after several heart-pounding attempts with no luck, I finally had to accept that I might never know.

But then, I had an a-ha moment. I realized that as difficult as this experience was, perhaps it didn't happen *to* me—but *for* me. I saw that it carried a hidden gift, it gave me a glimpse into something much deeper—how Erika must have felt as the driver in our family car accident. Though we've always told Erika that she wasn't to blame, she has carried immense guilt. Through this experience with the dog, I finally understood—in a way I never could before—just how *heavy* that guilt must feel.

Upon this realization, I called Erika and told her that I finally had a small taste of what she's lived with for years—the anxiety, the heartbreak, the fear of facing those who were hurt. Erika said that it was so painful to see Kristin and me in the rehab, and this experience gave me a better understanding of how that must have felt. Our conversation was very healing. I praised her strength, telling her what a brave soul she is. And I said something I truly believe: "Brian is still right here with us, and he orchestrates things in our lives to help us." The moment those words left my lips— ding—a text from my mom came through.

She was in a counseling session and she mentioned my accident, causing her counselor to recognize that the woman who had been walking the dogs was also one of her clients.

How was it possible that they shared the same counselor?

1985 – Erika, 10, and Brian, 3

The woman—Amberly—had just been in for support, as her dog, Lucy, had passed away. She was very worried about how I was managing but didn't know how to find me. With Amberly's permission, the counselor sent my mom her phone number.

How was it possible that we were able to find each other in this way? Brian—that's how!

When I spoke with Amberly, we cried together. I apologized and shared what I had learned. She said that our conversation brought her so much peace—and we both agreed there are no accidents. That call put an end to my sleepless nights, and I learned that her parents lived on the next street over—I had been searching on the wrong street the entire time.

Within less than a week of the accident, there was closure, connection, and healing—for all of us. Even in loss, Lucy's life had meaning. Her pain served a purpose—and so did mine.

The next day, my mom stopped by to give me a hug and we

marveled at the miracles that had taken place. Then my mom said: "Lucy in the Sky with Brian," likening it to the song "Lucy in the Sky with Diamonds," by the Beatles. Together, we shed tears as we pictured Brian taking care of Lucy until the day she is reunited with Amberly and her parents.

When a friend of mine heard about what had happened, she called and asked, "Of all the people in the world, why did it have to be *you* who hit a dog? You're such an animal lover." Without hesitation, I answered, "Of all the people in this world—it *needed* to be me."

Every time we face a trial, there is a lesson to be found. Because the hardest experiences are given to us as teachers. And, if we look for the lesson, we will always find it. If I hadn't looked deeper to find the lesson, it would have boiled down to just a tough experience, never realizing that it didn't happen *to* me—it happened *for* me.

Whenever you're faced with a challenging experience, I invite you to look for the lesson. Look for the miracles. And don't miss the gifts hidden in your trials—because they may be shaping you in ways you can't yet see.

18

KEEP THAT FACE

When I was in high school, some friends of mine were in a tragic car accident, just before our senior year in 1990. This was approximately one year before my family's accident. Unfortunately, Jeremy, who was one of the passengers, was killed—he was my secret crush. When I heard of Jeremy's passing, I didn't believe it. I kept thinking, "Are they sure he really died?" I was in so much denial, but when the reality of his death finally sank in, I was very sad, and I shed many tears.

One evening while I was in my room crying, Brian came in and handed me a note. He had drawn a smiley face with an arrow pointing to it that read, "Keep that Face," and "I hope you feel better." What a thoughtful little brother to be so caring! It meant so much, warmed my heart, and brought a smile to my face.

I think of Brian's words often, and they remind me to keep smiling. He would want it that way, as do all our loved ones. They want us to go on, to live our lives, and to be happy. They are happy, and we should be, too. When I think of Brian, I try to smile more often than I cry. Yes, we are left behind, and it's very painful because we miss them so much—but they still exist, and we will be with them again. It is okay to miss them, but it's important not to miss out on life.

It's interesting that Brian shared this message with me, just a year before his own passing, which has helped me so much. Several years after his death, I decided that my family needed his message, too, so I made copies, framed them, and gave each family member one as a Christmas present: "From Brian." I am so grateful for this thoughtful gift that Brian left behind—for all of us.

Several years ago, my sister Erika was asked to share her story in a blog that documents the journeys of strong people who have survived very difficult life trials. In the blog, Erika shared Brian's drawing and wrote the following:

"The time we have with our loved ones is unknown, so enjoy every moment to its fullest. This picture serves as a reminder that Brian is happy, and he wants us to smile. He wants us to 'keep that face' no matter what comes our way. This gift has given me a way to see the positive when things seem so negative. My brother Brian gave us this gift of hope and the gift of peace, so when I'm feeling down, I remember his words: 'Keep that Face,' and suddenly I start seeing all the things in my life that are worth smiling for." Years later, when Erika's kids were grown, her daughter Ashlyn loved Brian's message so much that she had "Keep that Face" tattooed on her arm.

PART III

FRIENDS + FAMILY

Over the years, I've found that when I tell others about the signs I've experienced, it opens the door for them to share their experiences with me. Talking about signs from our loved ones needs to be normalized, as it seems that receiving signs from beyond is much more common that we realize, but most people just don't talk about them.

I am thankful for the signs that other people have shared with me, as it builds upon my belief that these things are real and that they do happen. The experiences I share in this section are from people who I know and trust, who have also received signs from their loved ones, with a few signs from Brian sprinkled throughout. I'm honored to have been granted permission to share these very special and sacred experiences here.

19

MUSIC

Music is one of the easiest ways for our loved ones to reach us, because it's everywhere—in the car, at the store, in the gym, etc. If you receive a sign through music, it will *usually* happen on a special date that pertains to your loved one. Other times, the lyrics deliver a message that you need to hear, at just the perfect moment. Our loved ones have the power to influence music through various electronics: radios, iPods, and smart devices such as phones and speakers.

It is also possible to experience signs through electrical occurrences involving lights or devices such as clocks, computers, and televisions.

In October of 2022, my dad's girlfriend Teri left this Earth for the other side. She was the love of his life, and they shared a truly profound 15-year relationship together. After the diagnosis of a rare intestinal disorder, with little hope of recovery, Teri ended her own life. She decided that she could no longer continue enduring the unending prospects of daily suffering and pain for the rest of her life.

When my dad and Teri first met, they both lived in Utah, but after several years, she moved back to her hometown in California. Moving didn't interest my dad, as he was settled in Utah, and didn't want to move away from his three daughters. However, he and Teri continued their relationship, visiting each other periodically and talking over the phone every day, for hours on end.

Teri's passing has been completely devastating for my dad. In fact, within a month after her passing, his heart began stopping for long pauses during the night, which necessitated a pacemaker. She was who his heart had *beat* for, and she was who his heart now *broke* for.

In preparation for Teri's celebration of life, her family asked my dad if he would compile a visual tribute for the memorial, consisting of photos and videos, as this is one of my dad's special talents. He agreed, knowing that's what Teri would have wanted. Although it was a very emotional process to look through and assemble all the media, he did it, but only because of his immense love for her.

The very last video clip that he included was one that he happened to stumble upon before finishing. He had forgotten that he had this video and was happy to have found it. This video was filmed in my dad's home during one of their periodical visits, where Teri sang "Somewhere Over the Rainbow" to my dad. She introduced the song by saying, "This is for Tony, whom I'll love always and forever, with all my heart, for someday when I'm somewhere over the rainbow." She proceeded to sing a unique and unconventional version of the song, concluding it by blowing a kiss to my dad.

After my dad finalized the video compilation, he sent a copy to Teri's daughter, and she praised the video, saying that it was perfect, and would be the highlight of the memorial. My dad recalls, "That night, I went to sleep feeling proud that I had accomplished something important for Teri and her family."

Teri had left behind a goodbye note for my dad, along with several other sentimental items. In the note, she encouraged my dad to "Look for the number 3:44." They both considered 3:44 and 4:44 to be the same number because of the difference in time zones between them. Interestingly, 44s in general would show up for them at the most interesting and coincidental times, which they would discuss with one another in wonderment. My dad now refers to 44 as Teri's "signature number." My dad continued, "That night, I was awakened out of a deep sleep, and when I rose to check the time, my digital clock read 3:44." At that exact moment, his smart speaker began playing "Somewhere Over the Rainbow," covered by Katharine McPhee, which he had never heard before, and is a unique version similar to the one that Teri sang in the video. He sat in utter disbelief as the clock shined a bright 3:44, and the dark silence that had previously filled the room was now filled with the same lyrics that Teri had left behind. Both my dad and I are sure that it was her way of thanking him for completing the video, and I'm sure she was right there, blowing him a kiss.

After this experience, "Somewhere Over the Rainbow" and the number 44 have become Teri's signature signs for my dad. Since her passing, my dad has received many significant signs, but this one stands out to him the very most, and was one of the first.

When asked about his belief in the afterlife, my dad answered, "It is in my nature to be skeptical, as I am a trained engineer, but after that occasion, and the many others that have followed, my skepticism is now dust in the wind. Any previous doubts and questions of coincidence are gone. To have personally experienced such a profound happening, left me a believer: a believer that the core of who we are (light and energy, perhaps), and the love we have and share in this mortal life, continue forward."

A former coworker of mine, named Leanne, had an experience with her late father, 12 years after he passed from cancer. When she was a young girl, her father would sing "Edelweiss" from *The Sound of*

Music to her every night. After he passed away, Leanne kept the tradition by singing "Edelweiss" to her boys every night, telling them that it was a lullaby from grandpa.

After my time with Leanne in the corporate world, she became an influencer, fashionista, and seamstress—designing and sewing one-of-a-kind, jaw-dropping dresses. Several years ago, she decided to create one new dress every month, for a whole year, with the goal of taking them on tour. Once she had finished all 12, she traveled to event spaces around the country, displaying her gorgeous dresses for her followers to gush over.

Leanne shared, "Each night of the dress tour, I have felt so proud and so loved, but the sting of my dad not being here to see this, really hurt." A beautiful playlist that she had put together sounded in the background at each venue, as she conversed with her many followers. On the last night of the dress tour, as they were wrapping up, Leanne's husband took the opportunity to ask her to dance before they left the beautiful space.

Wearing a gorgeous light blue gown, she met her husband on the dance floor, just as the playlist ended. Knowing that Spotify will automatically play random songs once a playlist ends, they came together to dance to whatever might play. Emulating Prince Charming and Cinderella, just before the stroke of midnight, they began to dance as the next song swept them off their feet—it was the most beautiful version of "Edelweiss," and it felt like pure magic.

Leanne stated, "This was truly one of the closest times I've ever felt to my dad since he died. It was like he was there with me, telling me how proud he was. It was most definitely not a coincidence, and is a moment I'll never forget."

I will never forget her experience either, as it really struck a chord with me—bringing back all my memories of when Brian has played his songs at significant times. The timing of the sign Leanne received was so perfect, and it was as if her father had taken the place of the fairy godmother that night to applaud his daughter for her success—sending a hello from Heaven that she'll always cherish. To hear that song, at that time, was extraordinary, and couldn't have been more perfect.

My husband Shane had a friend whom he had known for decades, but they had lost touch over the recent years. In the summer of 2024, Shane was getting ready for work, while listening to the local radio station. On the radio, it was announced that his friend had passed away, as he was a well-known figure in the community. My husband was shocked by this news and felt very sad.

On his way to work, he ran a quick errand to return something at the store. When he arrived and stepped out of his car, the music playing on the outdoor speakers of the store made it apparent that his friend was saying goodbye. The song was "Breakout" by Swing Out Sister, which was released in 1986, and is quite rare to hear these days. Back in the day, Shane had introduced this song to his friend, who immediately purchased the CD, which became his favorite song and one of his favorite bands.

Over the years, whenever Shane has heard that song, it always made him think of his friend. Hearing the news and hearing the song, both within an hour of each other, is no coincidence. When Shane told me about this, I raved about what an amazing sign this was. My husband has been skeptical of signs, since he hadn't experienced any for himself—until now. Perhaps this sign was a gift from his friend, to move him one step closer to becoming a believer.

As a family tradition, my friend Jenny and her family would go on an annual camping trip every Labor Day Weekend to Fort Bridger, Wyoming. Jenny's father Dennis had a deep love for American history and loved visiting the historical sites each time they went there. In August of 1997, Dennis passed away, only a week before their annual trip, when Jenny was just 18 years old. In his remembrance, Jenny and her family kept the tradition alive. The week after his passing was no exception, as Fort Bridger had now become a place where the family could continue feeling close to him.

Later that year, as the very first Christmas without him was approaching, Jenny's brother Kenny decided to dedicate a song to their father, as a special gift to the family. He chose to learn the song "Love, Me," by Collin Raye because the lyrics felt like something his father would say. He performed it for his immediate family, right on Christmas Day, which has made this song hold special meaning for all of them ever since, reminding them of their father.

The following September, Jenny, Kenny, their two sisters, and their mom traveled from Utah to Wyoming for their traditional trip to Fort Bridger. Neither Jenny, nor her siblings, had families of their own at the time. During their drive, "Love, Me" played randomly on the car radio. As soon as it began playing, all of them knew that it was a sign that Dennis was right there with them, and they were all deeply touched. For the next 17 years, only some of the family continued going on their annual trip to visit Fort Bridger, always traveling in the same car, and each year, that song would play on the radio during their drive to the campsite. Not just one or two years, but this happened *each* of those 17 years since Dennis's passing! As we all know, thousands upon thousands of songs play on the radio every day. For that special song, which was dedicated to Dennis, to play *every* time they drove to the campsite, is an undeniable sign to all of them that their father is still with them.

20

MESSAGES

I believe that before we come here to Earth, we set intentions for reaching certain goals. When we get off track, sometimes Divine Spirit will give us little nudges to push us in the right direction by sending us messages.

These messages can be sent externally through other people, or internally through the mind—which is telepathic and is how communication takes place on the other side. When sent externally, the messages can come either directly from someone else, or through a conversation that you overhear. When sent internally, the message will pop into your mind, almost as if the thought was downloaded from somewhere else and is clearly not your own.

For example, when my heart needed attention, I heard the message, "Do it now and it will be repaired," and when the nurse wasn't allowing me to speak with my cardiologist, I heard the message, "Call after hours," and I immediately thought, "Good idea!" which made it obvious to me that I hadn't generated that thought. Pay attention to the thoughts that come to you from seemingly out of nowhere—those are messages and guidance from the other side.

Divine Spirit knows the goals we chose to achieve during this lifetime—they see the bigger picture. They have access to the entire map with all the mile markers we set out to hit along our journey, while we can only see the road directly in front of us. When we are lost, Divine Spirit can redirect us back to our intended path by sending us messages.

Shortly after the accident, my mom joined a bereavement group, led by her counselor, for mothers who have experienced the death of a child. During one of the sessions, a message came into my mom's mind that said, "She is your mentor." This caught her off guard, and she wondered where this thought came from, as it was clearly not one of her own, and came through very sharply. The message was confusing, as she couldn't imagine what her counselor might mentor her on. Immediately, the message came through again, even more sharply the second time, so she decided to sit with it and see what might happen.

Not long after this, my mom's counselor offered her a scholarship to become certified as a hypnotherapist. Because of the message she had received, she decided to accept, mostly out of curiosity. As a bonus, her counselor ordained her as a Universal Life Minister, which gave her the authority to officiate weddings. My mom practiced as a successful hypnotherapist for several years, but never thought she would ever officiate a wedding, as she does not like public speaking. However, when she mentioned to a friend that she was ordained as a minister, she was asked to officiate her wedding. She accepted, and was hooked!

She has now conducted almost one thousand weddings, and it's been the most fulfilling career path she could have ever dreamed of. My mom is so thankful that she listened to the message she received that day, because her counselor most definitely became her mentor, and led her to what she was meant to do.

~

During the "grunge" era, I had a boyfriend named Troy, who I dated from 1995–1999, and he was the walking definition of the word. He worked in the music industry, was the lead guitarist and singer in a punk band, and although I had long hair, it felt short in comparison to his, which flowed all the way down his back, reaching his waist. Wherever he'd go, the batting of eyelashes would follow. The minute I saw him, I fell in love with him and his bad-boy image, but it didn't take long to discover that we didn't share the same values and goals. Deep down, I suspected that these differences would lead to the eventual demise of our relationship. But I buried my suspicions deep inside and swept the red flags under the rug, because I wanted it to work so badly. I tricked myself into thinking that if I tried hard enough, our differences would eventually resolve.

His band played often, and I attended all of his shows. I loved watching him in his element, and quickly got used to the groupies, which was just part of being in a band. I was very supportive of him, but over time, he demonstrated that his groupies were more important to him than I was.

During one of his performances, time suddenly seemed to move in slow motion—it was one of the most surreal experiences that I've ever had. During this slowed moment in time, I took a good, hard, look at everything that was going on around me, and it was not a good scene. In this moment, an extremely clear message came into my mind: "You don't have to live like this. Your life could be so different." This thought was clearly not my own.

Despite our issues, I was all-in on this guy, and breaking up with him had never crossed my mind as an option. The fact that this message was given in second person by using "*you*" rather than "*I,*" was extremely significant in affirming to me that it came from somewhere other than myself. The message was pivotal in waking me up from the daze I had been stuck in during our relationship, and helped illuminate the fact that I was not being valued. This occurred in a smoke-filled, hole-in-the-wall dive bar—which goes to show that guidance from Divine Spirit can happen *anywhere*.

Upon hearing the message, my first thought was, "You're right!" which was shocking to me. I knew I had a decision to make, but I was torn because I loved him. During his next performance, he kissed a girl while onstage. This surpassed the flirting, and I was not okay with it. The fact that this kiss lasted 10 of what seemed to be the longest seconds of my life made it even worse. Later that night when I expressed how I felt, he discounted my feelings, saying it wasn't a big deal. He told me that I was being "too sensitive," which I had come to believe after hearing this from him so many times during the past four years of our relationship.

Not long after this, a mutual friend of ours could see that I was having a hard time, and he told me, "I can't tell you anything specific, but I will say that he's not treating you right." It was extremely validating to hear this from a male perspective, and I finally admitted to myself that I knew it was true. When I told another friend of mine, Lauren, that he'd kissed a girl onstage, her immediate reaction was, "Did you kick his ass?"

Standing at six-and-a-half feet tall, Lauren could have easily been a supermodel, turning heads the minute she walked into a room. She was truly a punk-goth goddess and rocked her style like only she could, never taking crap from anyone. She was a total badass—and if a badass like her wouldn't stand for that kind of behavior, then why should I? Her comment helped me see that I wasn't being too sensitive—I was being gaslighted.

The words of these two friends were truly heaven-sent, and magnified the message that I had received during that surreal moment in time, which greatly influenced my pending decision. After sitting with my feelings and the messages I had received, I dug deep inside myself and exhumed the early suspicions that I had buried about our differences. It became very clear to me that I had been choosing someone who wasn't choosing me back, and I knew that it was time to choose myself. It was painful to realize that our puzzle pieces just didn't match—he wasn't the one for me, and I wasn't the one for him. I knew that it was time to step away from my state of stagnation and into a state of freedom, by living my life, instead of his.

So, I traded in the red flags for a white flag, and surrendered our relationship. I stopped trying to make the relationship what I wanted it to be, and finally saw it for what it was—and it was no longer what I wanted. I wanted more, and I knew that I deserved more. So, I said goodbye, and learned what true heartbreak felt like. Everyone in my life could hardly believe that I broke up with him, and to be honest, neither could I. It wasn't easy letting go of someone I loved, but I had to—because I knew that putting myself first was long overdue.

I know that Divine Spirit guided me to this decision, which completely changed the direction of my life. I had thought that this relationship was what I wanted, but Divine Spirit knew better, shining a spotlight on the truths I needed to see, and redirecting me to a new path that I was brave enough to take.

About a month later, he wanted to work things out, but I didn't let the roses he carried sway my decision. I finally knew my worth, and I stood firm in not going back to someone who didn't value me. I gained respect for myself through this process, and because I stood my ground, I believe that he finally gained respect for me as well. Although at first, I was angry with myself for staying with him for as long as I did, eventually I recognized the many lessons I learned from that relationship—the biggest one being to stop seeking love outside myself, and to instead find it *within*. When you learn to love yourself, you quit putting up with bad treatment—and my first steps towards self-love were leaving him, and not taking him back. I also learned not to invest in someone whose values and goals don't align with mine, and instead of continuing to be angry with myself, I gave myself grace for not surrendering sooner.

Ultimately, this painful ending eventually led me to a new beginning. Over the next few years, I went on to make some new boyfriends and some ex-boyfriends, and I know that Divine Spirit led me to each of those relationships so I could learn the lessons that were necessary for my growth.

In 2017, my sister Erika was having one of the most difficult times of her life. She was contemplating a divorce, and was very hesitant to leave her marriage of 20 years behind. Signatures were yet to be written, and the thought of having her family broken apart was torture.

One afternoon, as she was in her car feeling emotional about her predicament, she received a notification that a CD was on hold for her at the library. When she picked it up, she was taken aback when she saw that it was a blank CD with the words "It will destroy you," written on it. Because her marriage was no longer in a good place, she knew that it meant staying with him would destroy her. She then went to the bank to sign a check, but the pen wasn't working, so she pulled a piece of paper off a pad provided by the bank, to scribble on, which had the bank's logo and slogan on it.

What she had unknowingly underlined as she scribbled, were the words, "You can." She was amazed by this message that seemed to cheer her on. Her next stop was the grocery store, and all the lyrics of the music playing over the speakers were about walking away and standing on your own—they were just what she needed to hear. She said, "Surprisingly, I didn't recognize any of the songs, but all the lyrics really stood out to me, as they were about ending relationships and moving forward."

She then heard a message in her mind that said, "It needs to happen," which she had heard multiple times before. However, being the one to move forward with the divorce was tearing her apart inside, which made her feel paralyzed in doing anything about it. Hearing the message again that day, along with the other affirming messages she received, convinced her that divorcing was what she needed to do. Later that day, to her astonishment, signed divorce papers were delivered, awaiting her signature. This all happened on the same day!

Getting divorced was very painful, but it ended up being a positive thing in her life. She has grown so much and is now happily remarried to the love of her life. She feels that God gives family members on the other side the responsibility of helping their family members who are still here, and recalls, "I feel that Brian was with me the whole time and was the one guiding me. He came through for me by sending multiple messages to really get the point across."

Also in 2017, my sister Kristin was in the same predicament that Erika was in, as she was contemplating leaving her marriage of 20 years, as well. She simply didn't know what to do. In hopes of gaining clarity, she prayed, asking God to give her guidance as to whether she should get a divorce. She then opened the scriptures, and the first verse she began reading had the word divorce in it. Feeling guided, she was able to proceed. Soon thereafter, she and her husband gathered their children together to tell them they were getting divorced. It was one of the most painful experiences that Kristin has been through.

As tears flowed from everyone's eyes, Kristin's heart was breaking—it was such a dismal scene. As this was happening, she suddenly felt as if a protective bubble surrounded her, which created a separation from the sadness. She felt overwhelming peace and heard the words, "You are doing the right thing, you are doing the right thing, you are doing the right thing." She feels that this message, and the guidance she received, came from God, and describes this experience as being "very sacred."

Although her divorce was very difficult, she says, "If I had stayed in the marriage, I wouldn't be the person I am today." She is so grateful for the immense growth she has gained since the divorce, as she has been able to witness her own strength and has learned to stand on her own. A mantra that she lives by now is, "Life is always working in our favor—always." Interestingly, both of my sisters got married the same year, divorced the same year, and both marriages lasted 20 years.

Donna, my dear friend who saw the glow around Brian the day before he died, lived in her home for decades, which she and her husband Ralph raised their seven children in. After Ralph passed away, Donna's children really wanted her to live closer to them, and they didn't want her having to worry about maintaining such a big home and yard.

So, Donna and one of her daughters went to look at a condo that checked all the boxes on their list. As they were looking around the condo, Donna heard a message in her mind that clearly said, "This is where I want you." A minute later she heard the same message a second time. She knew that the message came from her late husband, and she signed on the condo that very day.

In September of 2020, I consolidated my Facebook friends list so I could be more intentional with my social media usage. The following morning, I heard a name in my mind that was so clear I could almost see it. The name belonged to someone who I had unfriended the night before—a guy who I had known from elementary school, but hadn't seen or interacted with since. I immediately checked Facebook, and there was a friend request from him, awaiting my response. I was shocked as to what had just happened, and felt like I had just received a nudge from Divine Spirit, for a reason unbeknownst to me.

I trusted the coaxing and accepted his friend request. As I looked through his page, I noticed that he was a life coach, and his relationship status was "single." The thought of setting him up with my sister Kristin immediately popped into my mind, but I brushed it off. Day after day, I kept hearing the message, "Set them up." I hadn't interacted with this guy since elementary school, so I was hesitant, because I'm protective of my sister. Yet, I couldn't deny this message. So, I lined them up and never heard the message again.

They went out a couple of times, but realized they were better off as friends. However, Kristin loved his outlook on life so much that she decided to hire him as her life coach. During their sessions, he guided her through an intense course of personal development, which gave her the tools she needed to better navigate the world of single motherhood. This changed the way she had been looking at her life, and through this, she learned how to be content with being alone before seeking out a partner.

His coaching made a profound difference in her life, and everyone in her circle witnessed the transformation she made from caterpillar to butterfly. Kristin and I both agree that the gentle prods I received were divinely guided. Divine Spirit knows so much more than we do--we just need to be open to receive the messages and have the faith to follow them.

A few days after my friend Jen's grandmother passed away, she and a friend were together as Jen drove during rush hour. They were traveling north on the I-15 freeway, at the point of the mountain, which is the meeting point between two counties in Utah: Salt Lake County and Utah County. At this time, there were only three lanes. Jen recollected, "We were in the middle lane, and as we approached the top, at an incline, the road began curving towards the right." She described the freeway as "wall-to-wall cars," and felt her anxiety rising as she tried to navigate through the traffic, while thinking about how much she missed her grandmother.

Just as the road began to curve, time suddenly seemed to slow down as she heard the message, "Get over!" This message was not her own, and was repeated three times—the third being so strong it felt like a command. Directly in front of them was a huge semi-truck carrying extremely long logs, which were chained to an open trailer and stacked as high as the cab. In this moment Jen heard, "Trust yourself," and knew that she needed to get over, but they were surrounded by other vehicles.

Suddenly, she felt like someone took over her hands and jerked the wheel to the left. Her friend screamed as their car moved over to the next lane, and miraculously, there weren't any cars next to them. In the next moment, the chain that held the logs broke, causing the logs to tumble out of the truck bed to the right side. As the car curved with the road, Jenny recalls "The logs were rolling out as I was passing the truck—it was so scary and surreal." Jenny and her friend then looked behind them to see that the logs were falling all over the road, setting the stage for a horrific accident behind them. Jen is certain that they would have been killed if her car hadn't moved over to the next lane. She was in shock, but she knew that her grandmother had divinely intervened. They both could smell the scent of roses, which her grandmother loved, and felt her presence. As time began to speed up, her friend exclaimed, "Your grandma just saved us!"

One day in 2024, just as my dad was stepping out of the shower, he was surprised to hear a message in his mind that said, "Check the clock." The message was very clear, and it was not his own. He followed the prompting and stepped into the next room where his clock read 7:44. If you recall, my dad's late girlfriend Teri's final note to him said to "Look for the number 44." As my dad stared at the clock while shaking his head, he realized that the song "My Girl" was playing on his smart speaker. This song was very significant, as Teri would often tell my dad, "You'd be so proud of your girl." Although this sign was not life-changing, it was a way for Teri to wave hello, and I am glad my dad was able to receive her wave by following the prompting.

21

PHYSICAL SIGNS

Our loved ones can give us physical signs. These symbolic signs can be sent through nature—such as seeing a rainbow, animal, butterfly, or bird, at just the right time. They can also be sent as objects—such as coins, feathers, or heart-shaped items in your path. Our loved ones can send us gifts, can grab our attention by shattering glass, and can even touch us.

HEARTS FROM HEAVEN

In the summer of 2024, my dad and Erika went on a trip to the Oregon coast. One evening, as my dad rested in the hotel room, Erika went for a walk on the beach by herself. As she walked along the sandy shore, she asked Teri, "Help me find a perfect heart so that I can bring it back to my dad," while envisioning stumbling across either a heart-shaped rock or seashell. Heart-shaped items are considered signs from loved ones, dating back to ancient times, as the heart is the seat of the soul and represents affection, connection, and support.

After walking for about five minutes, with no hearts in sight, she turned around and began her way back, feeling discouraged. As she walked through the sand with her head hanging down, directly in her path laid a tiny perfect heart, facing upside-down.

Her eyes widened as she picked up the dime-sized wooden heart. The fact that she was able to spot this heart was incredible, as it could have easily been buried, and the light brown color of the wooden heart was camouflaged by the color of the sand.

The grains of sand lifted, as she blew on the heart, revealing the word LOVE inscribed into the wood! This reminds me of the coin-shaped copper pendant that my daughter found with LOVE carved across it. Erika's heart filled with awe, delight, and excitement as she looked down to where the heart had been. She dug around, and discovered three more identical hearts, just waiting for her to find them—making it a total of *four* hearts, which was profound, as it represented my dad and his three daughters. Out of an entire beach full of sand, she found *exactly* what she had asked for, and not only one heart, but four of them, to bring back to our dad!

The day before that happened, she and my dad had been talking about how Teri had lost her dad when she was a young girl, at age 10. My dad told Erika he has no doubt that Teri wants him to be here for his girls, as it was very hard on her not to have her dad around throughout her life. It is evident that Teri was listening to their conversation, and tuned in to fulfill Erika's wish, which signified so much in just four little hearts. When Erika shared her experience with my dad, and later with Kristin and I, we were all completely mind-blown.

After returning home from Oregon, my dad found a local jeweler to make the hearts into beautiful pendant necklaces for the four of us. The jeweler encased each one in glass, bordered by 14 karat gold—making them keepsakes for each of us to eventually pass on as heirlooms, and to keep this amazing experience alive and in our hearts. What a special gift from *both* my dad and Teri. To emphasize exactly how small these hearts were, and how difficult it would have been to spot them in the sand, please reference the dime next to the necklace, in the photo below.

I grabbed a stray dime from my coin jar for this photo, and had to do a double take when I saw that the year on the dime was 1982! This was the year that Brian was born! Receiving this 82 showed me that Brian and Teri are working together in the afterlife, even though they had never met in this life. Sometimes signs are so surreal that they can be hard to believe, and we question our own eyes. But I promise you that the dime I grabbed was completely random. This was a true "wow moment" for me.

BIRDS + BUTTERFLIES

When I was pregnant with my daughter, I would go out into the backyard *a lot* with my son, who was just a toddler. Once spring arrived, there was this little robin that would sit in our large dawn redwood tree, all alone, just watching us—every day. I had a strong inner feeling that this robin was either being influenced by my unborn daughter's spirit, or she had entered its body—to visit and watch over us before she arrived in her physical form.

Although birds are considered signs from loved ones, in general, the idea of an unborn child's spirit visiting an expectant mother in the guise of a bird, is a spiritual belief held by many indigenous cultures. This is derived from the symbolism that birds can act as messengers between the dimensions of the physical and non-physical worlds. Native American tribes interpret these visits to pregnant mothers as offering comfort and representing connection to family. Although this robin could have just been a robin, many cultures see robins as symbolizing new life, and I just had an uncanny *knowing* that my future daughter's spirit energy was working through this bird.

My son and I would say hello to the robin, and I felt a reassurance in seeing the bird every day, as it brought me a sense of peace that the birth would go smoothly, and my daughter would arrive safely. It also caused me to reflect on the pre-birth memory that I have of seeing my mom before I was born. I've always felt I chose my mom, and by seeing this robin every time we went into the backyard, I thought perhaps my daughter was choosing me, as well.

When I went into labor, my dad arrived at the hospital to take pictures and video of my daughter's first breaths and our introduction to her. Later, he compiled the media, along with music, into a beautiful keepsake for us to cherish. Once we viewed it, I was astounded to see that at the very end there was a photo of a robin, that looked just like the robin who had been watching over us every day. I asked my dad about the photo, and he said, "When I arrived at the hospital, there was this cute little robin sitting near the entrance of the hospital, as if it were waiting for me, so I took a picture of it and thought it would be fun to add to the end of the video." When I heard this, it confirmed my feelings that my unborn daughter had been visiting me as a robin! I truly feel that she was at the hospital in bird form before being born, as spirits can be quite fluid with how they direct their energy. I think it is amazing that my dad was inspired to take its picture that day and included it in the video, when he had *no idea* that a robin had been visiting us for months before the birth occurred.

A few days after arriving home from the hospital, I ventured into the backyard with my son and my new little daughter, and for the first time that season, the robin wasn't there. We never saw the robin again, which solidified to me that what I had felt was true.

In many cultures, rainbows are also believed to be signs from loved ones, symbolizing hope, promise, and reassurance that our loved ones are in a place of peace. My friend Amber received two signs from her brother Brandon, on the very day she learned of his passing. As she and her husband were driving, a turkey suddenly emerged in the middle of the road. They were able to come to a complete stop, and the turkey paused directly in front of their car. The turkey turned and looked at them, then proceeded to walk away.

Amber was stunned, because this sign was extremely significant for her, as she would often tease her brother by calling him "Turkey." She noted, "I had only seen a wild turkey in Utah one other time, and that was up in the mountains." Then, as her second sign, her brother sent a rainbow to greet them when they arrived home from their drive.

~

My friend Carolyn's mother-in-law, Jonia, lived in a cottage on Carolyn and her family's property for seven years, when she was not in good health. They cherished those years together and were very close. Her favorite color was yellow, and she was absolutely obsessed with flowers—she was the epitome of the saying, "Stop and smell the roses." Every Mother's Day, Carolyn gave her a gift of flowers by planting them next to Jonia's cottage.

Sadly, Jonia's declining health resulted in moving her to an assisted living center, in the dementia ward. As her health continued to deteriorate, Jonia's family came to say their last good-byes. Despite being a Christian and having a deep love for God, she was extremely fearful of death. She had stopped eating and drinking for nine days, but still had not passed, which reflected just how fearful and reluctant she was to leave.

So, her son offered a special prayer, after which Carolyn and her sister-in-law, Laura, lovingly massaged her with magnolia oil. Laura felt inspired to use this oil, saying, "I awoke with a distinct vision of a magnolia flower, which for me represents divine dignity. I instantly knew I needed to place this essential oil on my mother, as her oil of departure—sending her off dressed in dignity."

As the vapors from the oil ascended around them, they asked, "Mom, we know your love for us is so strong, and that you will still care for us from the other side. What kind of sign will you send us?" Their question was met with the answer, "Butterflies." When a loved one is close to death, it can be an optimal time to pre-establish the specific signs your loved one wants to send. However, if you didn't get the chance to ask your loved ones in person, you can still ask them in spirit, at *any* time.

As their eyes filled with tears, they said, "Mom, *you* are our butterfly." As she took her very last breaths, they continued, "It's okay to go—fly like a butterfly! Be free and spread your wings to that beautiful place where Dad is waiting for you."

It is beautiful that Jonia chose butterflies as her sign, because the metamorphosis from caterpillar to butterfly perfectly represents the transformation of the soul—leaving the body and the physical world, and rebirthing into spirit and the afterlife.

After Jonia's passing, Carolyn was the main organizer during the funeral and had many duties to fulfill—likening her role to "being the mother of the bride." Among her duties, she played the prelude music as guests arrived; sadly, because of this, she missed the opportunity to be there when the family gathered to pray and close the casket, just before the funeral began. She yearned for that much-needed closure of saying goodbye and holding Jonia's hand one final time.

After the burial, she went to get groceries for all the family she was hosting. As she left the store, she asked Jonia, "Were you pleased with today and the way we honored your life and love for all of us?" Just then, as she walked towards her car, she grew concerned when she noticed that a van was following her. Upon reaching her car, she nervously began loading the groceries as the van pulled up behind her and a woman got out—walking straight towards her. Carolyn's breath was taken away when she saw that this woman was carrying a bouquet of bright *yellow* roses! The woman explained that she had a feeling that Carolyn needed these flowers. A complete and utter stranger, delivering a gift that perfectly represented Jonia on this very emotional day—this was her answer…Yes! Jonia was most definitely pleased with today! Although Carolyn had missed saying goodbye one last time, this experience brought her the closure she needed.

Carolyn then grabbed one of the photos from her car, which had been displayed at the funeral, explaining to the woman that this was her mother-in-law, and that her funeral had just been held that day. The woman was awestruck to see that the photo revealed a woman holding a bright yellow flower inside of a frame, lined with yellow, hand-painted flowers.

The woman then shared that this was the anniversary date of giving her child up for adoption, and every year since, she honors her child by purchasing flowers and allowing herself to be guided as to who needs to receive them. This year, she was guided to Carolyn. This woman is an excellent example of trusting and surrendering to the nudges from Divine Spirit. She was open enough to receive the message, present enough to hear it, and brave enough to follow through.

The following Mother's Day, Carolyn stepped outside to visit the flower patch she had planted for Jonia. She missed her terribly and spoke out loud, saying, "Mom, I hope you like the flowers." Just then, a huge, yellow tiger swallowtail butterfly, about the size of her hand, fluttered up and landed on her chest. The butterfly stayed there for a good moment before fluttering away. Jonia had told her that butterflies would be her sign, and in this moment, she proved it to Carolyn, leaving no doubts in her mind. This butterfly was not only a sign, but a gift, and what an incredible and special gift to receive—especially on Mother's Day.

When Carolyn shared her experience about the butterfly, it reminded me of a Netflix docuseries I had watched a few years earlier, called *Surviving Death*, which premiered in January 2021. Episode #4 titled, "Signs from the Dead," features many different people talking about the signs they've received from departed loved ones. In this episode, a woman asked her dying mother for one last request, saying, "Send me a cardinal when you get to Heaven, and I'll know you made it," just like Jonia told Carolyn and Laura that she would send a butterfly as her sign.

The day after her mother's service, the woman and her sister were playing a card game and heard a bird hit the window. They ran outside, and to their great surprise, the bird was a cardinal. One of them picked up the bird and was delighted when it sat contentedly in her hands. She encouraged the bird to fly, but it was at ease just resting in her palms. It eventually flew to her shoulder and sat there for quite a while, just like the butterfly did with Carolyn, until it finally flew away. This was all caught on video while it was happening and is shown during the episode. I am sure that our loved ones fly free, just as birds and butterflies do, once they depart from this physical existence.

SHATTERED GLASS

In November of 2022, a month after my dad's beloved Teri passed, and shortly before he had to get a pacemaker implanted, my sister Erika was in her kitchen, when suddenly, she heard glass shattering. She looked at the dishrack sitting on her countertop and was stunned to see that a glass lid now sat in pieces. The lid was the only object in the dishrack, so there wasn't anything nearby that could have caused it to break.

Teri was very strong-willed, and Erika knew, without question, that this was a sign from her. She interpreted that it meant she needed to give our dad a call. She immediately said out loud, "Okay Teri, I'll check on my dad."

Erika continued, "Earlier that day, my son had seen a woman quickly walk past the bathroom door. He thought it was me, but I was nowhere near the bathroom door. In fact, I was upstairs, and my son's bathroom was downstairs, and nobody else was home except for us. Again, my first thought was: Teri is here. I had been feeling her presence all day, so the shattered glass felt like she was trying to get my attention."

Erika called to check on dad and he assured her that everything was fine. But later that day, Erika and I spoke, and I revealed to her that he had told me his heart had recently begun stopping during his sleep. Erika recalls, "Once I knew that, it was obvious that Teri was worried about him, and even though we know that she longs to be with dad again on the other side, she chose to get my attention so we could encourage dad to get a pacemaker, helping to prolong his life, so he could be here with us." All three of us girls then encouraged our dad to get a pacemaker, and the next day, he did.

While a scientific phenomenon known as "spontaneous glass breakage" *can* occur in glass, it is extremely rare. The physical reasons for this are either due to thermal shock, which is a rapid change in temperature, or manufacturing defects, such as nickel sulfide particles expanding within the glass. In this example, there had been no rapid change in temperature, and while it's very unlikely to have a manufacturing defect, the chances of a glass lid breaking due to this and without any external force, are especially slim. Because of Teri's love for my dad, and the worrisome situation he was in with his heart, my family and I recognize this as a sign.

TOUCH

Even though our loved ones are no longer in the flesh, they can use their energy to let their presence be known. Their energy is very powerful. They can place objects in your path, tip over heavy items, manipulate radios and smart speakers, and can even use their energy to create the sensation of touch.

I grew up with the cutest little lapdog named Gizmo, whom we called Giz. He was a mix of cocker spaniel, chihuahua, and poodle, and was the sweetest thing. Whenever my family and I would visit our grandparents, we would bring Giz along with us, and whenever we went out of town, he would stay with them. He loved visiting them, and my grandparents loved having him. We cherished our time with him for 15 years before he went to the other side in 1999. Giz brought so much comfort to my siblings and I after our parents divorced. He was not just a pet—he was a truly beloved family member.

A few years after his passing, I stopped by my grandparents' home for a visit one afternoon, during a break I had in-between my college classes, in 2002. As we sat at their dining table and visited, I felt a sudden and undeniable warmth on my lap that covered both of my thighs. It was so warm that I immediately looked down to see if something had somehow spilled on me.

The air conditioner kept it very cold inside their house, and I was wearing shorts, so the warmth was truly unmistakable. When I saw that nothing had spilled, my first thought was, "Giz!" When he was alive, he loved to sit on my lap, covering both thighs—precisely where I felt the warmth that day. I was so grateful for this sign. Later that evening as I got into bed, I spoke out loud to Giz, to thank him for the experience. It is important to give thanks when we receive signs.

My friend Gwen had never received, or asked for, any signs from her beloved Grandma Betty, who had passed seven years earlier. She really wanted to seek a connection with her, and felt inspired to try and ask for a sign. She began praying that her Grandma Betty would send her a sign—specifically asking for birds. During this time, she had a friend who was in a custody battle, and asked Gwen to testify in court. Gwen wanted to be there to emotionally support her friend, as she knew it was going to be a very stressful day for her, so she happily agreed to testify and attend the hearing.

During the proceeding, Gwen was sitting behind her friend and could see that she was crying. As her friend cried, in her mind, Gwen pleaded, "Oh, Grandma Betty, please be with my friend *right now*! Please be right next to her, and support her!" Later, as they drove home, Gwen's friend told her, "Before the session, I asked for all my departed matriarchs to be in the courtroom today. I could feel where they all were in the room, but I wasn't sure who it was that gave me the warm, comforting hug while I was crying. I actually turned around to see if it was you who was hugging me."

"That was my Grandma Betty!" Gwen exclaimed. "I asked her to comfort you when I saw that you were crying!"

Her friend agreed, saying, "Yeah, it was! Because I could tell where all the other grandmas were, and hers was a new presence, but a beautiful one." When Gwen shared this experience with me, I immediately reflected on the day when I had felt my dog's warmth touching my legs. It is truly amazing that it is still possible to feel the comforting touch of our loved ones.

Within the next thirty minutes, Gwen and her friend witnessed a surprising number of hawks, falcons, crows, sparrows, starlings, and even a Western Meadowlark fly directly in front of their car. Birds were special to Gwen and her grandma during their relationship on Earth, and she discovered they are still special to their relationship, even after Betty's departure.

Gwen received the signs from beyond she had hoped for, and discovered that you *can* ask your loved ones for signs, and they can step in and offer comfort when needed. Not only was Gwen there supporting her friend, so were all the grandmothers. Just because our loved ones no longer live in the flesh, they can still support us just as much in spirit.

I had a boyfriend named Greg, who I dated from June through December of 1994. During the six months we spent together, he was very critical, possessive, and controlling. One of the ways in which he tried to control me was the way I spoke. He wasn't fond of me using the word "like," the way a Valley Girl would say it. Anytime I would say it, he would harshly tap me on the top of my head, with one finger.

This made me feel like a toddler who was being scolded for saying a bad word. When I look back, it's clear to me why I didn't leave him after his first attempt to control me—I didn't fully love myself, but I do now. My younger self put up with a lot of things that I would never put up with now—or ever again.

Greg eventually decided to temporarily move back to his hometown, located in the Midwestern United States. Once he arrived, he tried to convince me to drive from Utah, located in the Western United States, to come visit him during the winter. Because of the control he had over me, I considered it, but I eventually ended up refusing. I really didn't want to see him, and not long after he moved, I summoned up the courage that I'd been suppressing for the past six months and broke up with him over the phone.

I wanted to end things sooner, but I was afraid. His move ended up being permanent, but despite our relationship status, he continued calling for several months. The conversations were never positive, and I asked him to stop calling, which he didn't, so I eventually quit taking his calls. During some of our phone conversations, he made threats that made me feel unsafe. I didn't know if he was joking, serious, or just trying to scare me. I tried to push his remarks into the back of my mind as I moved on with my life.

His threatening comments stayed buried for decades until one night, upon boredom during the COVID-19 lockdown in 2020, his comments resurfaced, and I decided to look him up, hoping to find that he was still living out-of-state. My search led me to a website called "Find a Grave," which pointed me to a headstone engraved with his name and birthdate.

In my search, I discovered that he was linked to a woman named Camille. I found her on Facebook, and it turned out that she was his ex-wife. On her page, I came across a post with a picture of her and two teenaged versions of Greg, standing over a headstone that matched the one I had just come across. In the post, she wrote about how much her sons missed their dad. Bingo—it was indeed Greg.

In that moment, I flashed back to a couple of years earlier, in 2018, when I had had a very strange experience. I was home alone, doing the dishes, when I felt a startling and harsh tap on the top of my head. I immediately touched my head, in hopes of feeling the remnants of a drop of water from Brian, only to be disappointed. It really felt more like a piece of hail had hit my head than a drop of water. So, I put my question out there into the Universe, asking, "Who is here? What are you trying to tell me?" The silence in the air was a bit unsettling, knowing that someone beyond my perception was there. My eyes searched the kitchen as if I were looking for Waldo, but I eventually turned around and continued doing the dishes.

I was going through a health scare at the time, which made me consider the possibility that someone on the other side was trying to get my attention for those reasons. Ultimately, it was a mystery, and I was left with bewilderment.

Fast-forward to the day that I discovered Greg had passed, and the questions I had from that strange experience were finally answered, and I knew it was Greg who had tapped me on the head. There could not have been a more distinct way for him to let me know it was him, because it felt *exactly* the way that he used to tap my head! At the time that it happened, the thought of it being Greg never crossed my mind, because I assumed he was alive. But now that I knew he had died, there was no doubt that it was him. I looked up and chanted, "like," to blatantly rebel against the way he used to control me.

Because there is so much learning that happens in the afterlife, I believe that he has let go of his ego and now understands how his actions impacted me. At the time, his tap was far from soothing, but once I realized that this tap was from him, I felt that this was his way of making amends, which is comforting. I am so grateful to have received this sign, as it is just even more reason for me to believe in the afterlife.

I then reached out to Greg's ex-wife, Camille, explaining who I was, while offering my condolences and admiring her strength. I let her know that I had a few pictures of Greg that I could send her to share with her sons. She gladly accepted and thanked me for reaching out. She shared that Greg had taken his own life, at age 41 in 2013, just three years after they divorced—they had been married for 10 years. When I felt the tap on my head, it was 2018, which had been five years since his passing. I was saddened to hear that he had taken his own life, but I was overwhelmed with relief at the same time. No longer would the space in the back of my mind need to carry the worry of him choosing to act on the threatening remarks he had made.

22

SIGNS DURING SLEEP

When loved ones visit us during sleep, this phenomenon is referred to as a "visitation dream," but don't let the word "dream" fool you. These "dreams" are not to be confused with the typical dream, as they are notably much more than just a dream. They feel more real than waking life, are *extremely* vivid and clear, and are very memorable—they don't fade away, unlike regular dreams that are fragmented and fade away within moments of waking. In this type of experience, your loved ones will appear in their prime, as the best version of themselves.

If a visitation dream is experienced around the time of a loved one's death, it's considered a shared-death experience (SDE). This often involves sharing in a loved one's transition into the *initial* stages of the afterlife, and can happen while sleeping or awake, and either remotely or at the bedside of a dying person. SDEs are said to greatly reduce the grief of those who experience them.

VISITATION DREAMS

When I reached out to Camille, she also shared that approximately one month after Greg's passing, she was awakened by the very strong scent of cigarette smoke. She stated, "He smoked like a freight train, and I knew it was a sign."

She then fell back to sleep and experienced a visitation dream. Her exact words were, "I saw him, but he didn't say anything—yet I knew what he was telling me. He was saying, 'I'm sorry.' We were communicating without speaking." This was a very validating detail, as communicating mind-to-mind is commonly reported in near-death experiences. Then she felt the most beautiful warmth that she has ever felt in her entire life. She described it as "pure happiness and bliss." The blissful feeling lingered after she woke up, and she knew that it was Greg's way of letting her know that he is okay and is finally at peace.

In January of 2018, a friend of mine named Lisa, who was also my neighbor, eventually lost her long battle with lung cancer that she had been fighting for almost six years. A few days after her passing, I had a dream where Lisa was holding her hands near the sides of her head, moving them back and forth, as if she were telling me something very exciting.

She was happy, healthy, smiling, and her porcelain skin was literally glowing from the inside out—she was beaming. I didn't have any recollection of what our conversation entailed, but I know that the topic was good because of the happiness that was emanating from her face. Looking back, I believe that we were communicating telepathically. She was dressed in pink, and even her cheeks seemed to be radiating a beautiful rosy color that came from within. Interestingly, one of her favorite colors was pink, which I found out when I read her obituary.

Almost seven years later, I was speaking with a friend and neighbor of mine named Leticia, and she told me that she had a visitation dream with Lisa the day before Lisa passed. I hadn't told her about my experience with Lisa, and I thought it was so interesting that we *each* had a dream with Lisa. I found it extremely interesting that Leticia's experience happened *before* Lisa passed. This demonstrates that when someone is very close to death, they have one foot in this life and the other foot in the next—allowing them to leave their body and communicate in spirit elsewhere.

In Leticia's visitation dream, she was standing off to the side of a paved road, when a fancy limousine came driving towards her and stopped. To her surprise, Lisa stepped out of the back of the limo. Leticia recalls, "She was wearing a dress and seemed calm, like she knew where she was going." They shared a hug, and Lisa reassured her that everything was going to be okay, while smiling during the entire experience.

They had been partners in a church calling, and had become close friends. Leticia had never lost a close friend before, so this was a new type of loss for her. She was so grateful for this gift of comfort that Lisa had given her, which really helped with easing her grief.

After Leticia shared this with me, I shared my experience with her. I don't think it was a coincidence that we spoke on this day. It was such a comfort to us both.

My Aunt Sheila passed away in June of 2023, after a challenging battle with liver cancer. Her obituary described her as having a "larger-than-life, 'firecracker' personality," which pretty much sums her up.

We had been close in the past, but in recent years, we were not. Even so, it didn't change the fact that I love my Aunt Sheila, and I know that being on the other side has allowed any grievances she held to dissipate. The day after her passing, I asked her for butterflies as a sign—specifically yellow or purple, since in many cultures, butterflies are considered a sign from departed loved ones, and represent transformation and new beginnings. I was hopeful that she now had a more positive disposition than the last time I saw her, and I felt that a sign from her would affirm this. Over the next two days, I came across three different posts on Facebook with pictures of butterflies, all of them being a combination of yellow and purple. My family and I went shopping for new dress clothes, to wear at her celebration of life, and to my delight, the girls' dressing room was filled with butterfly décor. Only a few weeks after her passing, my family and I took a trip to the mountains, and as we walked past an area full of rocks, a single yellow butterfly sat on the rock pile, fluttering its wings as if it were waving hello.

A couple of months later, I had a visitation dream from my Aunt Sheila. During this experience, I was at the reception center, where decades ago, my grandparents had celebrated their 50th wedding anniversary. This reception center doesn't exist anymore, but in this experience, it was like I had gone back in time. There were many people there, yet I didn't recognize any of them until I reached the top of a large staircase and found my Aunt Sheila conversing with my Aunt Ann, who had passed many years earlier.

I apprehensively touched Aunt Sheila's arm, not sure of how she would react because of the way our last interactions were, but I was relieved when she turned to look at me with a bright smile. She was in her prime, looking young and beautiful, and said, "Don't take things so personally." I found her comment especially interesting, because I had been working on trying not to take things so personally, especially after the last few times we'd seen each other, so this was an extremely pertinent message for me to receive from her.

The following week, the book club I attend announced the next book we were going to read. The subject of the book was about personality types called Enneagrams, so I ordered a copy and began reading. As I read through the characteristics of each personality type, there was one that perfectly described my Aunt Sheila. In that description, I came upon a sentence that stopped me in my tracks, stating, "When dealing with this personality type, try not to take things personally." I had to do a double take of the words on the page, as they were the same words that Aunt Sheila stated during the visitation dream! The fact that I had this dream *before* I even knew of this book was very significant to me. The dream and the book were two independent confirmations relaying the same message: don't take things personally. I now view my aunt as having been one of my teachers in life, teaching me not to take negative interactions to heart. I've also learned that the things that trigger us are spotlights, shining on the characteristics we need to look at within ourselves, and therefore work on.

The following March, in 2024, as I was getting ready for the day, Aunt Sheila crossed my thoughts. Our loved ones are always close, but when the thought of a loved one spontaneously comes into our minds, it means that we are simply tuning in to their presence. I then decided to ask her for a butterfly, once again. In my mind I said, "Aunt Sheila, please send me a yellow or purple butterfly sometime within the next two days."

That evening, my husband and I went out to dinner with some friends. Afterwards, we walked around town and did some window shopping. We walked past an antique shop, and in the window sat a small picture frame containing a real taxidermic butterfly with purple shaded wings! As they walked on, I stayed behind to snap a photo while thanking Aunt Sheila for this beautiful sign. A few months later, I decided that I needed that butterfly, as a reminder of the magical signs my aunt had given me. I hoped it hadn't been purchased, and to my delight, it was still there. It is now displayed on a shelf in my living room, and I think of her every time I see it.

SHARED-DEATH EXPERIENCES (SDES)

One night, in April of 2001, during my sleep I had a vision that a handful of men were walking towards me. They were all wearing the same thing: white button-up shirts with black ties, and black-framed eyeglasses. This was how my Uncle Wayne dressed, and in the center of all the men was my Uncle Wayne. The scene looked just like a clip from a movie—it was zoomed in, and I only saw them from the waist up, marching closer and closer. The experience only lasted a couple of seconds, yet it was very vivid and clear.

The next morning when I awoke, my mom announced that Uncle Wayne had passed during the night. I had never been close with him, and at the time I didn't know what to make of it, other than it was interesting. Because of the studying I've done, I now know that this was an SDE because this happened the night he passed.

I have often wondered why Uncle Wayne came to me when were weren't particularly close. Maybe we were close before we came to Earth, or perhaps he knew that I'd be receptive to the experience. There's also the possibility that he could see into the future and knew that I'd eventually share this experience with a wider audience.

In February of 2016, my husband, kids, and I flew from Utah to California to visit the happiest place on Earth—Disneyland! We checked into the hotel, and then goofed around Downtown Disney before going to bed early, as we planned to hit the parks at the crack of dawn. I went to sleep that night anticipating a fun-filled vacation with my family. As the moon disappeared, the room filled with excitement as our kids opened their eyes with the sun. But I awoke feeling perplexed, as my mind ruminated on the dream I had just awoken from.

During my sleep, I had been immersed in an all-encompassing light that seemed to have no beginning and no end. The characteristics of this space reminds me of "the void," but instead of darkness, it was full of light. In this vast whiteness, to my right, was my ex-boyfriend Troy, the one who epitomized the word "grunge." He was standing next to a woman with long, dark hair who looked to be in her early 30s. I sensed that they were on the verge of leaving, so I asked, "How do you two know each other?" The woman playfully answered, "Oh, from here, and from there," which gave me the impression that they had known each other for a long time.

In this experience, my son, who was seven years old, was to my left, and as I was patting him on the shoulder, Troy relayed to me, "You're a good mom." This was very significant, as he was acknowledging the fact that I had become a mother. As you know, in my past, I didn't express any interest in having children, and he was adamant against having them, as well.

This dream was so vivid and real, and I questioned why I had dreamt about him, especially since our relationship had ended over 17 years ago. Upon awakening, I felt a very strong sense of his presence on my right side—just as he was during the dream, which I attributed to the dream I had just awoken from.

My family and I went on to enjoy Disneyland, but I couldn't shake the feeling of his presence. After a long day of trekking through the parks and being whirled around on rides, my daughter's battery had fully drained, so she and my husband walked back to the hotel. Somehow, my son was still fully charged, so we stayed and played until the lights went out.

While we were leaving the park, we held hands as we shuffled down Main Street. My son was on my left, just as he was during the experience, and I let go of his hand when my watched buzzed with a notification. I was surprised to see a message from a woman named Jenna, who I hadn't heard from in years, and who was a mutual friend of Troy's. She wrote, "Hi, Karin. I'm not sure if you heard, but Troy passed away last night. My sister told me today... they aren't sure what happened, but he was found in his home."

The moment I read those words, I knew that this dream had been Troy's way of saying goodbye, and that it was more than just a dream—it was an experience. Because this happened the night he passed, it is considered an SDE. When I reflect on the experience now, I wonder why it hadn't entered my mind that he might have passed, but it didn't. I was out of my normal element, on vacation, and I was simply left puzzled by the whole experience.

Although I was shaken by the news, I wasn't surprised, as he had many health issues and died of natural causes. This experience showed me that he still exists, and it reinforced what I already believe—that this life is not the end. Not long after hearing the news, his presence began to dissipate.

Back when we were dating, I sat in his room one evening while he played guitar, and a clear message came into my mind. The message conveyed that he wouldn't live a long life and to soak in the moment, which I did.

The sting of his death was lightened because of the visitation dream, which is a wonderful gift that people who experience SDEs have reported. The fact that I had *already* grieved the loss of him when our relationship ended so many years ago, also helped. When a relationship ends, it's like a death and can be just as painful— sometimes even more so. We had dated for over four years, and it was my first significant relationship; therefore, it meant a lot to me that he came to say goodbye, which brought me a lot of peace.

After realizing that this was more than just a dream, I thought about the woman and figured that she must have been Troy's Spirit Guide. However, I have since learned that during SDEs there is often a "Conductor," who helps manage the transition into the afterlife, which is a term coined by researchers at the Shared Crossing Project. The dying may request to visit certain people before completely crossing over, and the Conductor acts as an escort, facilitating their requests. Conductors differ from Spirit

Guides, as a Conductor's specific job is to arrange for final good-byes as they shepherd the dying into the initial stages of the after-life. Conversely, Spirit Guides abide with us throughout our lifetimes, watching over us and offering subtle guidance when we need it.

About seven years later, in June of 2023, I took my son, who was fourteen years old at this time, to get a haircut at the local barber shop. As I sat in the waiting room, the song "Lust for Life" by Iggy Pop began playing over the speakers, which was one of Troy's favorites. My mind was suddenly flooded with images of him jumping around on stage, wearing either his Vans or Converse sneakers, and whipping his hair around, while he and his band would cover the song. I found it interesting to hear this song playing in a retail store, as the lyrics are not family-appropriate. As the song continued, I thought to myself, "This song sure reminds me of Troy, but I wouldn't necessarily call it a sign," until—the following second when his name echoed loudly across the room as one of the barbers called out the name of their next client.

I then *knew* it was a sign. I had initially discounted it because it was just an ordinary day, and I didn't want to jump to any conclu-sions. However, on this day, when the barber called out his name, I was proved wrong.

This experience caused me to reminisce over the sign I received years earlier when I heard two of Brian's songs back-to-back on my iPod, and wondered if it was simply a coincidence. If you recall, I asked Brian to show me that it wasn't just chance, by playing "Somewhere Out There" next, which immediately played on the radio after I asked for it.

These are two examples of how doubt can creep in. Signs can be so astonishing that we sometimes question them, like I initially did in these two examples. However, in *both* of these scenarios, my doubts were cleared. This a great reminder not to doubt the signs you receive. If you receive a sign—trust that it is one.

23

NUMBERS

Our loved ones can reach out to us through numbers, which is very exciting because numbers are everywhere—clocks, billboards, road signs, receipts, TVs, license plates, and other everyday locations. When you receive a number as a sign, it grabs your attention and lets you know that you're not alone.

Numbers can be sent as two types: angel numbers, or numbers that are specific to your loved one.

Angel numbers range between two and four numbers long, and come in sequences as 1s, 2s, 3s, etc.—such as 111, 222, 333, and so forth. These numbers indicate that you are on the right path and are being watched over. Whenever I've been going through a transitional period in my life, such as pregnancy, hardship, or a breakup, I seem to look at the clock just as it displays either 1:11 or 11:11. Whenever this happens, I feel comfort in knowing that I'm not alone. My sister Kristin sees the number 33 often, and she feels it's a nod from Divine Spirit that she's being supported.

Numbers that are specific to your loved one include their birth date, death date, anniversary date, favorite number, or another number of significance: to either them specifically, or one that you both shared, like the number 44 which my dad and Teri share.

My family members and I have received many numbers as signs from Brian. The numbers specific to him are his birth month (6), birth date (29), his birth year (82), and the year of the accident (91). Although I've never received, or asked for, a 6, I have received the rest of his numbers, as you will see.

44

In December of 2023, my dad and I took a trip to Disneyland. The anniversary of the day that my dad and his late girlfriend Teri met, happened to fall during our trip. That morning, my dad put his headphones on and hit shuffle, hoping to hear some meaningful songs sent from Teri. I witnessed him lying in bed, with tears rolling down his cheeks, as he listened to the music. He wore his headphones long enough to hear three songs, and each of them happened to be songs that Teri loved. He shared this with me afterwards, and we both reveled in how amazing it was for those special songs to play right on their anniversary date.

Shortly after, we got ready and started our 10-minute walk to Disneyland. We talked as we walked, and suddenly my dad stopped in his tracks as I watched his eyes grow wide. I followed to where his finger was pointing and saw that a car was stopped in the middle of the street, as if it were waiting for us to notice it. My eyes matched my dad's when I saw that it displayed Teri's signature number, 44, alongside the entire car as 444-4444. Both of us couldn't believe our eyes, and we knew it was Teri's way of saying, "Happy Anniversary."

Two months later, I visited Disneyland again with my husband and kids. When we arrived at the airport, I noticed tons of cars with the same number plastered all over them, which made the previous experience even more significant—since that taxi service is so widely used, how was it that my dad and I only saw *one* during our entire trip? And we happened to see it right on their anniversary date. Once my family and I arrived at the hotel, we were given room 5444, and I felt it was a wink from Teri.

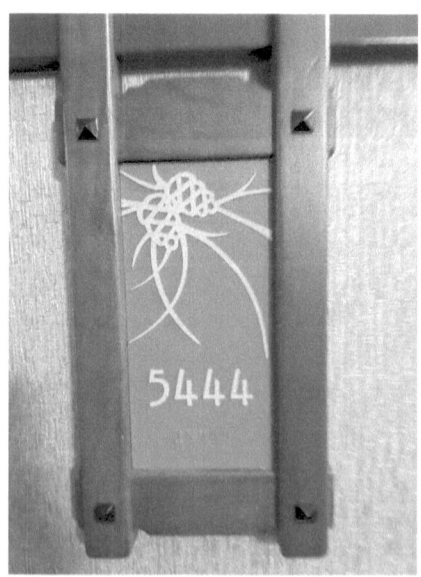

Ever since Teri's passing, there have been so many times that my dad has happened to glance at the clock, just as the minute is exactly 44, usually when he is thinking of her. Once, he was watching TV and his phone buzzed from an unknown number, only ringing once. The vibration caused his phone to slip from the arm of his chair, straight into his lap—displaying their *ultimate* number of 3:44, while staring back at him was Teri's picture that my dad keeps as his background photo. It was as if Teri was saying, "Hi! It's me!"

In February of 2025, there was a week when my sisters and I individually asked Teri for a sign, and were each awakened, on different nights, at exactly 3:44 am. *Each* of us—in the *same* week, with the *same* sign! Just like when my dad was mysteriously awakened at precisely 3:44 am and the song "Somewhere Over the Rainbow" began to play. These things are almost unbelievable, yet they are real.

29

In August of 2020, I was listening to a podcast about receiving signs from loved ones, and a father who lost his son was being interviewed—sharing that his son has given him, family members, and friends, signs with his favorite number.

His stories inspired me to ask Brian for a number, so I asked for a 29, to represent his birth date. As I continued driving, I knew that it could show up anywhere, and rather than scanning every license plate or road sign on the freeway, I simply trusted that it would come to me with ease. As I got close to home, just before exiting the freeway, a car merged directly in front of me, and there was my sign—the license plate had a 29 in it.

I shared this with my mom, and challenged her to ask Brian for a 29, as well. She took the challenge, and as she was exiting the freeway later that afternoon, she realized that all the exits near her home start with a 29 (297, 298), which she had never noticed or thought about before.

Our loved ones are with us, and we can talk to them and ask them for signs. Being present and taking notice of the sights and sounds around you can play a big part in receiving signs. My mom had never noticed the 29s on the exits near her home, until she became aware of the things around her and got present in the moment that day.

In November of 2020, my dad took a quick day trip to gamble in Wendover, Nevada, and the slot machines handed him a prize of five dollars. The roulette table sat empty, so he decided to play, betting it all on number 29—for Brian. When the roulette ball landed, 29 was where it stopped. The roulette dealer couldn't believe it and exclaimed to my dad, "To have someone walk up, bet it all on one number, and win on the first try—never happens!" My dad was astounded, and wished he had put much more than just the five dollars down!

82

In the spring of 2023, I was thinking about Brian and what type of sign I could ask him for. I thought about his birth year and decided to ask him for an 82—which has since become a number I ask him for often. Two days later, I was balancing my checkbook, and it was off by...you guessed it, *exactly* 82 cents! However, I had completely forgotten that I'd asked Brian for that sign. When I discovered that I was off by 82 cents, I recalculated to verify that my numbers were correct before I subtracted that amount from my balance. Once I had recalculated, it was *then* that I realized I had been given my sign! I had asked Brian for the sign on a Friday and said that I wanted it before the weekend was up. I balanced my checkbook right before bed on Sunday night, and received my sign just in time!

~

I attend a book club, and in the summer of 2023, one of the members, Kari, shared that her mom, Lousie, had passed away about a year prior. Two days before book club was Louise's birthday, and Kari had tagged her on Facebook to wish her a Happy "heavenly" Birthday. Even though her mom's account was no longer active, it was a nice way for Kari to send her a birthday wish. A woman who knew Louise commented on the post, saying that she had a bowl that Louise had made during a pottery class she'd taken many years prior, and wanted Kari to have it.

Kari picked up the bowl on her way to book club that evening, and was so happy to have received something that her mom had made—what a gift! The fact that this happened just a couple of days after her mom's birthday made it even more special.

As we were all leaving, we saw a gorgeous rainbow within perfect view. Kari shared that rainbows were a sign that she and her family recognized from their mom, so this was another perfect gift from her mom that day. We took group photos in front of the rainbow, and celebrated how amazing it was that these things occurred for Kari.

As we all began to leave, I shared with Kari that I had a brother who passed away many years ago, and I chose two of Brian's signs to share with her. The first sign I shared was when Finn the cat came at my daughter's request, and the second was the sign where my checkbook was exactly 82 cents short.

Right after I finished telling Kari about the 82, she said, "Hold on a minute; I need to get something to show you," and she ran to her car to grab the bowl her mom had made. When she approached me with the bowl, she turned it upside down, revealing what was etched into the bottom of it. I was astounded to see that beneath Louise's signature was the year '82!

It was pure magic to have experienced this sign together, right before both of our eyes, especially right after seeing that brilliant rainbow. This experience encouraged me to keep sharing my signs with others, and it also reaffirmed to me that our loved ones really are with us and involved in our lives. I found it interesting that of all the signs I could have shared with Kari that evening, I shared the sign about the 82, and she had just picked up the bowl with an 82 carved into it—I will forever be in awe over this.

A while after this experience, I asked Kari if she had ever

received signs from her mom. She said that one night she experienced a visitation dream where her mom said that feathers would be her sign. Many cultures believe that feathers, like birds, are a sign from our departed loved ones, as they represent ascension and offer reassurance to those left behind. In this dream, Kari explained to her mom that she wouldn't be able to pick up *every* feather she came across, and her mom said, "Well, maybe just the *special* ones," and then showed her a small brown feather that had a green tip. Kari shared this with her sisters, and one of them began seeing feathers all the time. Since then, Kari has found one special feather with a yellow tip.

During the week of Louise's passing, she received a rainbow every single day, and on the fifth day, there was a huge rainstorm, which is Kari's all-time favorite thing. This day happened to be a significant day, as not only was it Kari's birthday, but it was also the day of Louise's cremation. Her entire family felt that the rainstorm was a direct sign for Kari, giving her extra comfort on that difficult day, and acting as a birthday gift from her mom.

She told me that the experience we shared together inspired her, stating, "The new concept that you introduced me to was being able to *ask* for signs. I previously felt that you just sort of had to wait to see them, but being able to ask for them was a new idea for me."

Kari admitted that she's still somewhat hesitant to ask for signs, because she feels like receiving a sign is so special that you shouldn't ask for them too often. This can be a common reason why people hesitate to ask—but the more we ask, the more we receive. Asking is almost like sending a text to your loved one, which encourages them to respond, and sets the stage for your loved one to know that you'll be on the lookout, rather than hoping you'll notice. You can ask for the common signs, or you can ask for something specific—whether it's something you'd like to see, or something that reminds you of your loved one.

Another common reason that we may be hesitant asking for

signs, is the fear that your request won't be answered. While it's true that some people say they have never received signs, what's more likely is that there have been signs, but they either weren't recognized, the recipient wasn't open to the possibility of receiving them, or they never asked. Oftentimes, once a person starts receiving signs, they can look back into the past and realize they've been receiving signs all along, but just didn't recognize them at the time.

We will always be sent the signs that we'll best receive. One person may be less observant in waking life and more receptive during sleep, thereby receiving a visitation dream, whereas another person may be a great observer and easily recognize the signs that show up in their everyday life.

I'd been receiving nudges to write this book for quite a while. On New Year's Day in January of 2024, I had a rough outline done, and it was time to decide on either moving forward with it or laying it to rest. I asked Brian, "If I am really supposed to do this, please give me an 82 within the next two days." Later that day, I logged into my credit card account to make a payment, and the balance totaled $82.82! Not only did I receive my 82, but it was a *double* 82, which I felt was much more than a sign—it was a calling from my brother. I thanked him and embarked on the journey of sharing my story. I've felt his guidance throughout the process and am so grateful to have discovered part of my life's purpose through this calling.

 **Apple Card** Yesterday, 7:35 PM
Apple Card Payment Received
A payment of $82.82 was applied
to your Apple Card account
balance.

The following experience occurred after the book was published. It is so meaningful to me that I've included it here, as it relates to the story above.

I published the book in May of 2025. At the end of each month, authors receive a report showing the total number of books sold. When I reviewed the report for May, I was *astonished* to see that the total was 82.

The minute I saw the 82, chills covered my body, and I thanked Brian with all my heart. I truly feel that this sign is his way of saying, "You did it, sister!" It means the world to me and has reassured me of what I've sensed throughout this writing process—that he's been with me the entire time.

In September of 2024, I decided to ask Brian for an 82 again. I didn't have any special reason; I just wanted to feel connected to him. I wasn't seeking out my sign, as I didn't want to force it to happen— I just wanted to let it happen naturally. A week went by with nothing, until I pulled the grocery store receipt out of my pocket that I'd put in there earlier that day without looking at it. I was blown away to see that my total was *exactly* 82 dollars! What are the odds that every single item I purchased ended up totaling an even 82, after taxes? It was clear to me that it was a sign from Brian. If it had been mixed with other numbers like $71.82 or $82.56, it still would have been an amazing sign, but having my total come to an *exact* 82 was spectacular!

This deepened what I already knew—that our loved ones are

still right here. It caused me to reflect on all the signs with the number 82 that Brian has sent me, and how they've all been *straightforward* 82s: My checkbook was off by 82 cents, Kari's mom's bowl had an 82 inscribed on it, when I asked if I should write this book my balance was $82.82, and my grocery total was 82 dollars. I will forever be filled with amazement of how magical these signs are.

```
SMALL              4033           .36  1
       SUBTOTAL              79.49
       3.000% Food Sales Tax 2.31
       7.450% Sales Tax        .20
       TOTAL                82.00
CARD        TENDER         82.00
```

91

In the fall of 2023, I was waiting at a red light while thinking about how much my family and I have been through because of the accident. Sometimes it feels like it happened a lifetime ago, and that the person who survived it is a stranger, yet other times it feels like yesterday, and the experiences seem so recent and raw.

In that moment, I noticed a man across the street who had his back to me, wearing a white T-shirt with the year of our accident, 1991, stretched across his back! The strap from his bag covered most of the first number, but if you look closely, you can see it. I quickly took a photo, and it made my day. Sometimes signs just come out of nowhere, and being in the present moment and aware of your environment is so important.

SCENT

Receiving signs through scent is a very special and unmistakable way for a loved one to reach you. Although I haven't personally experienced this type of sign, I have family and friends who have. When this happens, the scent will be specific to our loved one so that the recipient will recognize who it's from—whether it be their signature cologne or perfume, their favorite flower, or the scent of something they enjoyed: cigarettes, coffee, food, etc.

My friend Donna, who I've mentioned before, said that the day she moved from her home to her new condo, she received a sign from her late husband, Ralph. As she sat down on the sofa in her new living room, the scent of Ralph's favorite cologne suddenly enveloped her. She then asked out loud, "Honey, are you here?"

The scent left her as quickly as it came, but without a doubt, she knew it was him. This only happened once, but it confirmed to her that she was in the right place, and that Ralph was happy that she had moved. She has been living there happily ever since.

Several years after my parents divorced, my mom dated a guy named Steve. He was a heavy drinker and smoker, and although my mom really liked him, she didn't desire that type of lifestyle, as she had grown up with parents who also drank and smoked. Although she truly cared for Steve, in the end, they put romance aside, but remained close friends. Unfortunately, Steve eventually passed due to heart failure in January of 2000.

On Steve's next birthday, March 29th, 2000, his kids invited my mom to celebrate with them at a restaurant, and she was honored to be included. As she was driving to the restaurant, her car was suddenly overwhelmed with the distinct smell of cigarette smoke, and she knew it was a "hello" from Steve. When she arrived, one of Steve's sons mentioned to her that he also smelled cigarette smoke on his drive there.

Not long after this experience, my mom was sitting at home, and for about 15 seconds, the scent of cigarette smoke surrounded her. She thought about who it could be, and felt that it was either Steve or her parents, as the smell of cigarette smoke would be a clear representation of any of them.

My friend Mike's father spent his final days in the hospital before he passed. Mike, his mother, and his siblings stayed in the hospital with him during this time and were all by his side when he passed.

Not long after his passing, they each began to detect the unique antiseptic scent of the hospital, even though they were no longer there. This scent reminded them of their father, and they all felt it was a sign that he was still with them. The scent would visit each of them whether they were together or apart, and whether they were inside or outside.

One afternoon as Mike, his mom, and his sister were getting into his car, one of them said, "He's here." Mike recalls, "We all smelled the aroma at the same time, and we knew he was with us." The scent would come and go at different times for over a month after his passing, until it finally dissipated. I feel that their father was especially close during that first month, to give them comfort when they needed him most.

EARTH ANGELS

From the examples I've shared, Divine Spirit can send us messages by way of signs, or through our thoughts. But, they can also work through others who act as earth angels, or messengers, to deliver communications that are much-needed by the receiver. Divine Spirit can work through others by inspiring their words and using them as a mouthpiece—making them temporary earth angels with a special delivery.

A particular experience stood out to me in the NDEs that I've studied. A woman had died in a hospital, and as she watched her body from above, she witnessed angels standing behind her doctor, leaning in, and working in synchronicity with her doctor's hands. Similarly, Divine Spirit can inspire and work through regular people's words.

In 1994, during the time that I was in the controlling relationship with Greg, I was able to break away one evening and go out on the town without him. I went to a bar that I used to frequent before we met, where I knew a lot of people. I was with a group of friends and acquaintances, and there was this guy in the group who I had seen once before but had never spoken to—until this night. As we were talking, he said to me, "You are perfect just the way you are." I was taken aback because these were the exact words that my soul deeply needed to hear at this time in my life, and it wasn't the kind of statement you'd typically get from someone you just met.

Like I mentioned, during my relationship with Greg, I was constantly being criticized. According to him, the things I liked were wrong—even down to the salad dressing I preferred, and he insisted that I do things the way that he did them. During the time we were together, I felt millions of miles away from anything close to perfect. So, hearing someone, especially a man, say those words to me was truly heaven-sent, and I knew that his words were divinely inspired. I never saw him again, but I was very grateful for this interaction and will always remember the words he shared.

My mom and I have always been close, and we get along very well. However, in December of 2020, we had a difficult conversation, which left my heart feeling heavy, and I know that hers was feeling that way as well. The following day, I went to the store and was feeling like a jerk for what had transpired between us. While I was out shopping, an older woman in a motorized cart was trying to grab something heavy from one of the shelves. I looked over as she was reaching for the item, and I ran over and asked if I could get the item down for her. She was delighted and exclaimed, "You are *so* nice! There are not many nice people in this world. My husband has six daughters about your age, and they are not very nice. You are a sweet girl." We were both teary-eyed at this point, and I genuinely thanked her as we went on our way.

Just the night before, I had spoken to Brian in my mind, asking him to help ease my heart. Of all the days for a perfect stranger to tell me that I am a "sweet girl," it was this day. They were the exact words I needed to hear at that time. I am sure that Brian worked through this woman to deliver the message I needed. I spoke with my sister Kristin about what had happened, and she agreed that Brian must have been behind it.

My husband and I attended a work-reunion picnic which was organized by some of his former team members, in the summer of 2023. He hadn't seen any of them in years, and I tagged along. They are all computer programmers, so most of the conversation revolved around their line of work.

I was delighted to see that my husband's former boss's wife, Dorothée, was there. She asked me what I was up to, so I shared that I was in the process of writing a book. At that point in time, all I really had was a rough outline. I had only told a few family members that I was beginning to write a book, so I surprised myself when I shared that with her. She asked me what the book was about, so I went on to tell her that the book is primarily about the signs that my family and I have received from my departed brother. I was telling her that sometimes we can get signs through other people and that when we receive signs from our loved ones, they are most likely to happen on significant dates—either on their birthday, or the anniversary date of their death. As I was sharing this, her eyes filled with tears. She explained to me that her mom had passed away about two years earlier, and that this day happened to be her mom's birthday.

Our conversation caused her to reflect upon that morning when she and a friend had met up to go on a hike. When they finished, her friend asked, "Did you know that today is President Nelson's birthday?" This caused Dorothée to reflect on her mom's past birthdays, as every year her mom would ask that same question, as she shared the same birth date as Nelson, who was the president of their church.

However, it wasn't until I mentioned that signs tend to happen on our loved one's *birthdays*, and can happen through *others*, that she realized her friend's words that morning were a sign from her mom. The words her friend said were exactly, word for word, what Dorothée's mom would say every year on her birthday. I know that our loved ones are aware of who we are with, and I can just picture her mom prompting both her friend, and me, to say what we did—using us each as earth angels: Dorothée's friend to deliver the sign to her daughter, and me to help Dorothée recognize the sign that she had been given.

In 2024, my friend Kreg and his sister had to make an incredibly difficult decision. Their mom had been living in an assisted living center with her husband (their stepdad), but her health had declined to the point where she needed to move to a different facility that could provide a higher level of care. This was not easy, as it meant their mom would be separated from her husband. Kreg and his sister never wanted to separate them, but unfortunately, it was necessary. They wished to have their stepdad move as well, but it was not up to them—that decision needed to be made by his children, and for whatever reason, they chose not to have their dad follow his wife to the other facility.

For the past 30 years, their mom had never been alone, so this was a significant change. After getting their mom settled into her new surroundings, Kreg had a panic attack on his drive home. He stopped at a nearby gas station to calm himself down and stated, "When I walked into the gas station, a little girl around the age of seven came up to me and handed me a folded piece of paper." To Kreg's surprise, he unfolded the paper to find the words, "Have a superb day!" This was a much-needed message for him to receive on this emotional day, and there is no doubt that the young girl was divinely led to deliver this message to Kreg that day.

It is amazing how Divine Spirit can work through others in delivering the messages that we need to hear, right when we need to hear them. If we can attune with Divine Spirit, by being open to inspiration that comes to us, we can also act as earth angels to others.

PART IV

LAST IMPRESSIONS

You have now read the story of my family's accident, the journey it took me on, and all the incredible signs that Brian and other lost loved ones have sent. While I've shared some glimpses of my life, I'd now like to share what happened after the accident, and how I'm doing presently.

There have been many miracles and life lessons learned. In these closing chapters, I share advice on dealing with grief and leave you with encouragement for getting your own signs, as I share what has worked for me.

MY LIFE

Life-altering losses are transformational, but whether they change your life positively or negatively, is up to you. I chose to quit walking the straight line I had walked all my life, and from there, my life took some twists and turns.

READJUSTING

I was still wheelchair-bound for a while after returning home, but not for long. I quickly moved to crutches, and soon I was walking. At that point, I took some time to readjust to life before returning to work and school. My friend Robert taught me how to play the bass, and we started a band with some other friends. The band didn't stay together for too long, but it was so much fun. I ended up starting college again for the spring semester of '92, and I went back to work just before summer began. These events comprised the next phase of my life.

NIGHTLIFE

In October of 1992, a year after the accident, I met a new friend named Sadie. We hit it off right away and quickly became best friends. We loved the nightlife, and went dancing at nightclubs every weekend, plus every Wednesday night. We also attended random concerts in-between. During one of our adventures, I met a guy named Ryan, and we ended up dating for over a year. Although we never made a formal commitment, I considered him my boyfriend. Alarm bells sounded when I noticed subtle differences in how they were acting, and I eventually pieced together that they had been seeing each other *behind my back*—for who knows how long. I had now become the casualty of two people falling in love.

Feelings of betrayal stung, and all kinds of questions ran through my mind. What hurt more than losing him, was losing her —she was my best friend, and a good friend doesn't do what she did! I felt so alone. My best friend was gone, and so was my boyfriend. What was I to do? I sat in the stillness, staring at my bedroom walls like a wolf who had lost its pack, wishing I was out enjoying the nightlife like I normally did with my best friend. It was then that I realized I had a choice: I could either grow old within my walls, or I could become my own best friend and go out by myself!

I felt comfortable enough from our previous weekends "on the scene" to venture out on my own. I recognized the gift in that, and what I initially saw as negatives, I now see as positives—such as gaining emotional resiliency, becoming self-reliant, and eventually landing where I'm at now. They say people are in our lives for a reason, a season, or a lifetime, and our time together had simply expired.

MY VICE

Around this time, I turned 21 and was of legal drinking age, and a whole new world opened up for me that I previously didn't have access to. So, I began venturing out to bars.

Although I'd never been introduced to alcohol before, some friends of mine made the introduction after my return home from the rehab. We would partake when we could obtain it, which was only a handful of times, but it was enough to discover that it drowned my sorrows and made me feel free. Once I could legally access it—it became my vice. Although I was very responsible with work and school, I was rebelling in other ways, one of which was being irresponsible with alcohol.

I soon became well-acquainted with the bar scene, and these establishments became my home away from home. I went out on the town multiple nights a week, and it was just the escape from reality that I needed. I quickly found my way around the clubs of Salt Lake City, and got to know most of the employees and the other regulars.

My best friend was no longer by my side, so alcohol and cigarettes became my new "friends." I had been caged by my shyness for so long, and alcohol was the key that freed me. It was the perfect recipe for liquid courage: simply mix any type of alcohol with one shy girl. I was binge drinking, roaming the bars—carrying each drink like a medal I'd earned.

Alcohol brought me out of my shell, morphing me into the outgoing person I had always dreamt of being, while also numbing the grief from the accident and the loss of my best friend. Sometimes I went out clubbing with friends, and although I enjoyed being with them, I grew to prefer traveling as the lone wolf I had become, because it allowed me the freedom to go where I wanted to go, and leave when I wanted to leave. I had come a long way from my middle school days of being so afraid to be seen alone, that I would eat my lunches sheltered behind a bathroom stall. But now, instead of hiding behind a stall, I was hiding behind alcohol. When I felt self-conscious about being alone at a club, I'd puff one cigarette after another, as I drank one drink after another, while a whisper of loneliness lurked behind my new "party girl" image.

During this time, I was lost, and I didn't know it—I was trying to find myself, and I was looking in all the wrong places. Who I had been was gone, and who I was yet to become, remained to be discovered. I'd been hiding behind the shadow of my shyness and following the rules of my religion for most of my life. Having come so close to death made me want to live, and I thought that drinking, smoking, and partying was living, but I was wrong. What I didn't realize was that I didn't need to do these things to live life—I needed to heal. I have realized a lot of things since then, and I can now see that deep down, I was angry and hurting inside, and the alcohol was the anesthetic that temporarily numbed my pain.

I have since learned that different types of traumas can lead to addiction, two of which are traumatic loss and acute trauma. Both boxes were checked by losing Brian in such a traumatic fashion, along with the acute injuries I incurred from the accident. Also, alcoholism runs on my mom's side of the family, which checked a third box. I'm not blaming my past alcohol use on these factors, but I know they played a part. I was stuck in a dark headspace, falling into habits that pulled me even deeper into the darkness.

FINDING MY LIGHT

I continued this lifestyle for almost 10 years, taking a four-year hiatus from smoking during that span. In the summer of 2003, when I was 30, I met up with some friends at a local DJ club where they spun house music, which I had recently begun listening to. It was a much-needed and refreshing change from the dark and angry music that I had been listening to for the previous 10 years. I was finally ready to look towards the future and leave that music in the past. House music was upbeat and happy—and I was ready to find my beat and be happy.

Halfway through the night, my friends decided to leave and go to another club. I opted to stay behind, in hopes that I'd be able to talk to this handsome guy who I had my eye on. I am so glad I went out by myself and didn't have to leave with my friends, because I did end up meeting him, and he changed my life. Looking back, I give a nod of gratitude to my experience a decade earlier with Sadie and Ryan, because the outcome led me to having the confidence to go out on my own, which eventually led me to this night.

When he introduced himself, I knew there was something different about him. His name was Shane, and we ended up talking all night. He also liked house music, and we came to find that we shared some mutual acquaintances and had similar backgrounds. He was easy to talk to, smart, and I felt safe with him. We began dating, and I had no desire to date anyone else, as I had a feeling that this guy was "the one."

After meeting him, I began to find my light as I came out of the darkness that I had been in for so long—I had been lost, and Shane found me. Shortly after we met, he began to DJ at some of the clubs, and I loved that we both enjoyed the same things. I'd still drink when we went out, but my binge-drinking days were behind me. Although I had smoked off-and-on for several years, I had quit for good, shortly before we met. Eventually, I grew to despise being around cigarette smoke, even helping with petitions to outlaw it in clubs. The petition was successful, and it was so nice being able to go to clubs without having to be around the smoke anymore.

Upon getting to know each other, we discovered that we had similar values and goals. However, there was one goal that we differed on, which was the desire for children. Shane really wanted children in the future, but because I didn't, it came close to throwing a wrench into our relationship. Even so, we fell in love, and after dating for over a year, Shane asked me to marry him.

We married in December of 2004, not long before my 32nd birthday, and Shane's 36th. Two years into our marriage, I was surprised that the desire to have children finally settled within me. After some introspection, I realized that my previous lack of desire for children was because I had been in relationships that I subconsciously knew weren't right for me. After adjusting to married life, I was finally in a stable and loving relationship where I felt safe to have children. We were both finally on the same page, and we looked forward to the next phase of our lives together.

MY PACK

My partying days had become a distant memory, and once we decided to start a family, I quit drinking altogether. Getting pregnant wasn't as easy as we had thought it would be, which was surprising, as pregnancy came easily to my mom and both of my younger sisters, so I assumed it would be the same for me. It took Shane and I a whole year to conceive, and we were so excited once we were finally expecting. We envisioned a whole new future, but sadly, six weeks into the pregnancy, I miscarried. It was a difficult time, but it showed me that getting pregnant was possible, while broadening my capacity for holding empathy towards couples who experience miscarriage.

Once we were ready to try again, it took another year to conceive, with fertility drugs this time around. I'm beyond happy to say that in 2009 we had our son, Ever. I knew that if I had a son, his middle name would be Brian. Before the gender of my firstborn was revealed, Shane loved the name Ever, for a girl. I didn't like that name for a girl, but when we found out that I was carrying a boy, I fell in love with the name because it honored my brother so perfectly: Ever Brian = Forever Brian.

After Ever turned one, we made the decision to start trying for a second child, as we didn't know how long it would take. In the meantime, Shane had created a fertility app that was inspired by our fertility struggles. By following the fertility predictions, in 2011 we conceived our daughter, Sola, in just four months, without the use of fertility drugs. We chose her name without even realizing it: Shane and I had seen the band Jamiroquai in concert before we had kids, and he told me the names of the band members; the percussionist's name was Sola. The second I heard that name, I said to Shane, "That would be a beautiful name for a girl." He agreed, and when we found out that our second child was a girl, we already knew her name.

We were thrilled to have her in our lives, and she completed our family of four. I finally had my pack!

I looked forward to having a drink once my body became my own again, but after I finished nursing both of my children, I found that my first long-awaited drink wasn't worth the wait. It wasn't the alcohol that had changed, it was me—I no longer needed that crutch to deal with my pain. I learned to *feel* my emotions rather than numb them. I began to love myself and stopped choosing to harm my body, mind, and spirit through alcohol. This shift became a turning point—allowing me to tap into my spiritual side and reconnect with Brian. From this new place of healing, my pain began to lift, and I started to receive more and more signs from him. I no longer drink because I choose not to, not because I'm told not to. To each their own. Cheers to those who drink responsibly, but as for me, I'll take a water.

Our children are now teenagers, and it's an exciting age, but parenting is not for the faint of heart. I now have two pieces of my heart existing outside of myself, which I'd do anything for, and will forever be concerned with.

In 2024, my son underwent an elective surgery, and afterwards, my husband and I were brought back to the recovery room so that we could be there once he woke up. When we were directed to the recovery area, there was a patient lying there, asleep with an oxygen mask over his nose. He looked so critical with the mask on, and I thought, "Thank God that is not my son," but then my heart dropped when I realized it was. Interestingly, my husband had those exact same thoughts. Our son was fine, but it was difficult seeing him lying there like that, and I realized this experience was giving me a small taste of how my parents felt when they saw me on life support after the accident.

One of the truest statements I've ever heard about parenting was from my dad when he said, "Children bring the greatest joy, and the potential for the greatest tragedy."

I was perfectly happy before motherhood, but having my kids in my life has changed my world and has taught me the meaning of true joy. It's difficult for me to imagine my previous mindset of not wanting children, because now I see that I was meant to be a mother all along. I just needed to wait for the right person and the right time. We all create our own timelines, and we all have unique stories and different paths to take. I got married when I was 31, and both of my younger sisters got married when they were just 19. They both had all their children before I was finished having mine —age 36 when I had my son, and age 38 for my daughter. I wasn't ready before then, and that's okay.

Two of my favorite quotes are, "Comparison is the thief of joy," by President Theodore Roosevelt, and "Comparison is the death of joy," which was later tweaked by Mark Twain. Both quotes are true, as comparison either steals your joy or kills it. Situations and circumstances simply cannot be compared, because yours is yours, and mine is mine.

Day by day, step by step, we each write our own stories. There is no need to rush ahead, and just because someone else is seemingly farther along, doesn't mean you're behind. Everything happens when it happens, and for its own purpose. Either way, our journeys are our own, and when we compare ourselves, we surrender our joy.

Presently, my focus is on being a mother and a wife, and now an author. As my children have grown, it feels surreal that they've already outlived the age that Brian reached, and are fast approaching the age that I was at the time of the accident. Several years ago, I surpassed the age that my parents were at the time of the accident, and when that time came, it was difficult to imagine being in their shoes. And now, 33 years later, sometimes it still feels as if it were just yesterday.

GETTING ANSWERS

To this day, I don't have any memories of the accident. But by speaking with the people who were at the scene, and carefully reviewing my hospital records, I was able to find answers to the questions that had swirled around in my mind for years.

As each witness drew from their memories, what they shared began to play like a film in my mind. A flood of emotions surfaced as I pictured what they described. At first, I wished I hadn't dug so deep, because what once had not existed in my mind, had now packed a bag to stay. Even so, I needed to understand exactly what had happened, and though it wasn't easy getting the answers, I am grateful to finally have them.

WRITING

In 2009, I created a private remembrance group for Brian on social media, uploading all his pictures, and inviting friends and family to join. I wanted a place where we could share our memories of him, wish him a Happy "heavenly" Birthday, and view pictures of him.

Every time I experienced a sign from Brian, I'd share it on his page, as would others. The first step I took when I began my outline for this book was to compile all the experiences that had been shared on Brian's page, and journal entries I'd written over the years. Both acted as a framework to get started, and it turned out that I had been writing this book all along. Even the poem I wrote in the rehab center, "Emotional Weather," became an integral part of the book's introduction, with the last line of the poem, "Bright days do come," becoming the title.

I am so glad that I've been documenting Brian's signs as they've happened—otherwise, some of the memories would have faded over time or been forgotten.

The process of writing about the accident, my recovery, and reflecting on the lessons I've learned has been emotional, yet therapeutic. Sharing these experiences has brought about a sense of purpose for my pain, and knowing that Brian has been beside me on this journey has been a real comfort. I want these stories to live on—to be remembered. My heart's desire is for others to know that life—and love—continue beyond death.

MIRACLES

Given all the injuries that I incurred from the accident, it is miraculous that I only have a few residual issues at this point in my life. These include my knee, shoulder, and one back rib (near my shoulder blade), all on the left side. Because my knee was fractured, the joint suffers from post-traumatic osteoarthritis. Running, down-hill hiking, or walking too briskly causes pain, as does keeping it too straight while lying down.

The injures to my shoulder and back rib cause them to be highly sensitive to stress and certain activities, one of which is driving on the freeway. When I am fully clothed, you wouldn't be able to tell that I'd been in an accident. If you saw my shoulder exposed, you might wonder, but if you saw me in shorts, you'd know once you noticed the scars on my legs. But, to be left with only these few complaints after such a life-altering accident is remarkable, and I count my blessings every day.

Speaking with the Mabeys made me realize, even more than I already did, what a miracle it is that any of us survived, and what a miracle it is that I have my legs and can walk. During our conversation, Dr. Mabey said to me, "Any time people are ejected from a car, the survival rates are not good. I fully expected that at least two people in your family would have died." I consider all the "happenings" to be miracles...Dr. Mabey happened to be driving directly behind us, he happened to have his medical kit with him, which happened to contain exactly what I needed (saline solution and a narcotic), he happened to be the only one who could successfully intubate me, and most of the volunteers happened to have medical backgrounds—the right people were there at the right time.

I've often thought about the fact that my kids were partially in the accident with me, since females are born carrying all their eggs. It is truly a miracle that my sisters and I were even able to have children. I am very fortunate to be alive, to be able to walk, and to have my children.

Also miraculous is the fact that my heart didn't incur any damage from being thrown. I already had mitral valve prolapse, and because my chest wall was hit hard enough to collapse both lungs, it's miraculous that my heart was somehow protected. Per my hospital records, the possibility of a valve rupture was the primary concern of the cardiologist who was on call upon my arrival at the hospital. Because of all these factors, it is astonishing to me that there was no rupture.

Something interesting occurred in 2018, almost three decades after the accident. I had an MRI scan of my abdomen, and the radiologist found something of concern that was outside of my reason for being there. He had great suspicion that it was a tumor, known as a GIST (Gastrointestinal Stromal Tumor), on my small intestine. GIST tumors are rare and make up less than one percent of all gastrointestinal tumors. I was immediately scheduled for the soonest available appointment with the top surgeon at the Huntsman Cancer Institute, who specializes in treating this type of tumor. I had no idea what my future held, and waiting for the appointment took a lot of discipline to keep my imagination from running wild. In the meantime, I was sent to have a CT scan so they could obtain even clearer images.

On the day of my appointment, the first thing the surgeon said to me was, "I've looked over your history and your scan results. Years ago, you were thrown from a car—is that correct?" "Yes," I replied. She went on to explain that it's not uncommon for the spleen to be impacted when someone is ejected from a vehicle; it can either rupture, or part of it can break off. What happened to mine was the latter. The spleen is located on the left side of the abdomen, so when the left side of my body hit the ground when I was thrown, a piece of my spleen broke off. The surgeon told me that it had even formed its own blood supply!

I never had any idea that my spleen had been impacted during the accident, and to discover this so many years later was shocking. A ruptured spleen is life-threatening and can cause substantial internal bleeding, which can lead to shock and potential death if it isn't managed in a timely manner. Because I was already losing so much blood externally, my body wouldn't have been able to handle losing more blood internally. I surely would have died if my spleen had ruptured. I am amazed that didn't happen. I am so surprised that the breakage was never discovered during the initial scans that were done upon my arrival at the hospital. Regardless, when I was told that there was no tumor, just a rogue piece of spleen, I was able to release a huge sigh of relief, releasing the worry that I had been holding during this time.

LIFE LESSONS

Opportunities that present themselves to us in life aren't always wrapped up in a bow, but they are indeed a gift. Initially, we often don't see them as such and aren't always excited about them— because they often pose as challenges, obstacles, and adversities. One of the reports in my hospital records begins with, "This unfortunate young woman…" If I had been conscious enough to agree at the time, I would have. However, I now disagree. Although the accident was tragic, it also bestowed many gifts. It showed my family and I just how strong we are, it woke us up to what's most important in life, and it led us to unwrapping the knowledge that our existence doesn't end with death.

In 2018, grief stopped by and tapped me on the shoulder as I was missing Brian and thinking about the accident. The radio was playing, and the main verse of the song repeated, "Let me out!" I realized that the accident had truly let me out from where I'd been hiding since I was a child. I felt like Brian was right there, directing my attention to this detail.

When I was a young "Screaming Kid," there was this expressive person inside of me that was shut down by water being splashed into my face, causing me to lock my self-expression away. Coming so close to death because of the accident helped me see that it was time to express myself again and not be afraid to live.

With every trial we encounter, a seed for growth is planted, which results in lessons learned. Life is really just one lesson after another, and the hardships we encounter can be used as fuel to transform us—if we let them. The things that break us can be the things that make us—but it is a *choice*. You can choose to see your trials as negative and end up broken. Or, you can rise above them and turn your wounds into wisdom. Finding the gifts that are hidden in our trials can take time, but through reflection, we can learn from the past and uncover the roses that we once viewed as thorns, which allows us to bring the insight we have gained through our experiences, into the future.

Through curiosity, we can start to find the gifts while we are in the midst of our storms. When you are going through a trial, ask yourself, "What is this teaching me?" and, "How will this help me grow?" Look for those seeds *as* they are being planted, instead of after they bloom.

GIFTS

Like a yin and yang, life has its ups and downs, positives and negatives, good times and bad. Although we often wish that everything was always good, duality is necessary to truly appreciate the full spectrum of life. The good times become that much sweeter because of the difficult times. If everything was always good, we might not appreciate it as such. Most likely, life would get boring, and we'd take things for granted.

Our periods of hardship spur our growth and cultivate an appreciation that didn't exist before that trial came along. Our adversities also bring a depth of understanding and empathy that we really can't get any other way. Imagine what your life would look like if you never experienced challenging things. Would you be the person you are today? I know that I am no longer the person I was before the accident. Life's storms are inevitable, and it's not easy when there is thunder and lightning, but the storms strengthen and mold us into who we are, so that we can shine even brighter than before.

It's almost as if we are born as shapeless lumps of clay, but experience after experience, and trial after trial, we start to take shape into the people we are today. The accident gave me shape and configuration, and I have found gratitude in what others might consider broken pieces. I've been able to put those pieces back together in a different way than before, and I've gotten something even more beautiful out of it—my whole family has. In hindsight, I now see that my trials were happening *for* me, instead of happening *to* me—they were gifts.

PERSPECTIVE

If you choose to look at the positives in life, there really isn't much to complain about. Keeping a gratitude journal has been something that has helped me keep a positive mindset. I write down three things every day that I am grateful for, and while it only takes a minute, the benefits are invaluable. Science has shown that keeping a journal specific to gratitude reinforces positive neural pathways, thereby rewiring the brain. It has also been found to bring about more emotional awareness, increase happiness, and decrease depression.

It will always hurt that Brian died, and I will miss him until we meet again, but I know that he is not gone. Instead of focusing on the fact that I only had my brother for nine years, I have changed my perspective to being grateful that I was able to have nine years with him. Nine short years, or nine long years—it's all about perspective.

I have always loved this poem, which relays a similar message:

REMEMBER ME

"Do not shed tears when I have gone,
but smile instead because I have lived.

Do not shut your eyes and pray that I'll come back,
but open your eyes and see all that I have left behind.

I know your heart will be empty, because you cannot see me,
but still,
I want you to be full of the love we shared.

You can turn your back on tomorrow,
and live only for yesterday,
or you can be happy for tomorrow,
because of what happened between us yesterday.

You can remember me, and grieve that I have gone,
or you can cherish my memory, and let it live on.

You can cry and lose yourself,
become distraught and turn your back on the world,
or you can do what I want…
smile, wipe away the tears, learn to love again, and go on."

—David Harkins

In every situation, there are always positive aspects to be found. If you haven't dug down deep to find them, I promise you that there is always some type of silver lining to be discovered.

For example, being the oldest, I always longed for an older brother, but now I have one, as Brian is my angel brother. He watches over me and my family, and even though he isn't with us in the flesh, he has shown us that he is with us in spirit. He can help us even more now, and can guide us in all kinds of situations. He is on call 24/7, as all our loved ones are.

LIFE IS SHORT

When you are young, you think you're invincible and that you'll live forever, but once you're older, you wonder where the time went and are grateful to see another day. I heard this analogy about time and death, and I've found it to be very true.

When you see an airplane flying by, it seems to be moving slowly, because you're far from it—like when you're young: you are far from death, and therefore time seems to move slowly.

But when you stand next to an accelerating plane heading down the runway, its speed is very noticeable because you're close to it—like when you're older: you are closer to death, and therefore time seems to accelerate.

Time is passing here on Earth, whether it seems to go by slowly or quickly. But what I've learned is that time works very differently on the other side. During my near-death experience, time seemed to stand still. Other experiencers have echoed this by saying that time doesn't exist there—which is hard to wrap our heads around while we are here in this earthly existence.

Remember how long it felt waiting for Christmas to arrive when you were a child, yet once you're grown up, it seems to come and go in a hot second? It's a funny, or not so funny, little trick that life plays on us. Life also plays tricks on us depending on the vantage point from which you're viewing your existence. When you project into the future, things seem so far away, but when you reflect on the echoes of the past, things seem like just yesterday.

None of us know when our last day will arrive, but one thing we can do to make our time here more comfortable is to take good care of our body, which is the vehicle that allows us to be here and experience this earthly plane. If you were only allowed one car to last an entire lifetime, you'd be sure to give it only the best fuel and take extra good care of it so that you could do the things you want to do. Our bodies are the same—we only get one. A quote that has always inspired me, by Joyce Sunada, is "If you don't take time for your wellness, you will be forced to take time for your illness." My great-grandmother Goldie, who drank carrot juice every day and lived to be 100 years old, always said, "If you have your health, you have everything," and it really is the truth.

LETTING GO

When I look back on my life, and reflect on lessons learned, I have no regrets. Yes, I've made some poor choices in the past, and I am not proud of everything I have done, especially my "wild years" of drinking and smoking. Nevertheless, those years are only a small piece of my story. I choose to let go of my past, and instead, focus on the present.

I love this quote by Victoria Holt, which reads, "Never regret. If it's good, it's wonderful. If it's bad, it's experience." Living in regret is no way to live. When we reflect on certain choices, we sometimes wish we'd done things differently, but we are here to live and learn. Every choice is simply a stepping stone in our journey. The only thing we should regret are the things we didn't do. So, my challenge to you is to do them now, while you still can. When you wake up each morning, ask yourself, "If today were my last day, what would I regret not doing?" Then, go do it.

Everything that I've been through has led me to where I am today, and I am grateful for where I've landed. My goal has been to be vulnerable and authentic in sharing my journey and my truths. I hope that these truths will serve you.

In addition to the life lessons I've shared, I want to stress how important it is to let go of grudges and resentments. The only thing that holding onto them will do for you, is to steal the richness from your relationships. So, let them go! Life can end at any moment, so make your interactions meaningful ones, and always leave people better off than they were before. Take a step back every so often, and imagine observing yourself in your everyday life. Think about how you want to be remembered, and then not only act that way, but *be* that way.

EXPRESSING LOVE

There are so many ways you can show your love to those around you. Simply sharing what you appreciate about others goes a long way in making the people in your life feel noticed and valued. If you don't say it, they won't know it. Don't leave things unsaid.

There are always opportunities to help others—look for them and don't let them slip by. Whether it's helping someone in need, doing something to brighten someone's day, or simply lending an ear. As I mentioned, in my prayers I ask for guidance as to where I'm needed, and therefore, I try to pay extra attention to inspiration that comes to me.

Acknowledge the strengths you see in others. Recently, I was in a store at a two-story mall on a busy Saturday. I noticed a blind woman enter the store, and I put myself into her shoes and saw how incredibly brave she was. I approached her, asking, "Do you know how amazing you are?" She thanked me, and I could tell that my comment really touched her. Although it was simply a comment, giving her that recognition was a way to spread some love.

This experience got me thinking about gratitude, and how I am so grateful to have my vision, but that I never really give it much thought, and because I've always been able to see, I take it for granted. On the other hand, I often think about how grateful I am to be able to walk, because I once couldn't, so I never take my ability to walk for granted. I found it interesting that once something is taken from us, after we get it back, we are grateful for it, but this interaction inspired me to be grateful for it all, not just for the things I once didn't have. When we live in a state of gratitude, we live in a state of love.

MANIFESTING

One of the life lessons I learned from the accident is to focus my energy on envisioning positive outcomes instead of negative ones. Earlier, I stated that I had often thought to myself that one of the worst things that could ever happen to a person would be to break both legs at the same time, and then it happened to me. I wondered if I had manifested this in some sort of backwards way. I really believe in manifestation: what we think about, comes about. Just like a photographer checks the focus just before taking a photo, let's make sure our focus is on the things we want to manifest in our lives, and not on the things we don't.

FINDING YOUR "WHY"

Lastly, discover your "why." We go about our days forgetting why we are even here and why we do the things we do. But if we can stand back and look at the big picture, we aren't here just to work, eat, sleep, and die. We are here for much more than that.

What is important to you in this life? What is the reason behind *why* you do the things you do? What you do today, creates your life tomorrow. Maybe you are right on track with your "why," or perhaps you need to re-evaluate what's most important to you, and what sparks your passion. Once you discover what your "why" is, it will bring a certain zest into your life, light a fire inside of you, and add joy to your days.

RELEASING GRIEF

Grief is defined as the emotional response to loss. It is one of the most difficult things we face in this life. When we lose a loved one, there is a part of us that dies along with them—because we both carry memories of one another that nobody one else does.

The grief surrounding the loss of Brian has always felt very surreal to me. In a way, I feel like I was robbed from the bereavement process because of the circumstances surrounding his death. Learning of his death after his funeral had already taken place, and returning home, months later, to find his belongings reduced to a cardboard box, was heartbreaking.

Once I was home, life began moving forward, and my grief buried itself under a litany of dark habits, such as alcohol and cigarettes.

Although I had plenty of physical and occupational therapy during my recovery, emotional therapy was forgotten. Decades later, in 2018, I finally got myself the therapy I had never received, which allowed me to feel and release many of my buried emotions.

Grief is not linear; it circles back around, but with each circle, the pain can soften a little bit. A zigzag going down a broken heart is an opening, and although the pain of our loss never completely goes away, if we allow ourselves to *feel* our broken hearts, it will help to *heal* our broken hearts. Each time we consciously experience our grief, it helps us heal—a little at a time.

By feeling our emotions as they come, we can learn to move it from the driver's seat to the back seat. The emotion of grief comes in waves, and when the waves of grief crash upon us, we should allow ourselves to feel them.

My mom describes grief in this way: "Imagine grief filling up in a glass (sometimes slowly, other times quickly). When the grief reaches the top, it spills over—causing tears to flow."

Shedding our tears when grief reaches the top keeps it from being stuck inside. Some may try to bury the pain inside, like I used to, but doing so can result in disrupted sleep, health problems, anger issues, depression, anxiety, self-destructive behaviors, substance abuse, and more. While it is important to allow ourselves to feel the waves of grief, we should not allow them to pull us out to sea for so long that we drown.

Take a minute to imagine things from the perspective of our loved ones who have left—they can see us, but we can't see them. They understand that we need to grieve when the waves hit us, but when they see us wallowing and living in the sadness day after day, it is painful for them.

Our loved ones want to see us living our lives. The best thing we can do is to smile more often than we cry when we think of them. Live for those you love, both living and dead, but most importantly, live for *you*. You are here *now*, and this is *your* life that *you* are meant to live.

THE LAST TIME

Grief may visit us when we realize that we've already had our "last time" with someone or something, such as spending time with a friend, getting a hug from your grandma, seeing your favorite band, tucking your child into bed, eating your favorite food, etc. There will be a last time for everything, but rarely do we know it's the last time while it's happening.

When you're at your favorite place, you think you'll be back, but what if that ends up being the last time? Savor each time as if it *is* the last time, because one day it will be, and none of us know when that last time will be. I never knew that day in the car would be the last time my body was whole, and I never knew that would be the last time I'd see Brian during this lifetime.

One reason that we don't savor things the way that we should is because we think there's more to come. With food, for example: if we have a plate full of food in front of us, we don't truly slow down and enjoy it because we know there's more—until we are down to the last bite or two. It's the same with life: we know we have more time—but what if we don't? Don't wait until the end to savor life; savor it now. Experience each moment to its fullest, and as each moment goes, the next one comes, and each one is truly unique.

Tomorrow is not promised to any of us. Life is finite, precious, and fragile, and I've been given the opportunity to learn this first-hand. The accident helped me realize how short life truly is, and helped me see that it's much too short not to say the things you want to say and do the things you want to do. I urge you to wake up to this fact now—before something forces you to wake up.

EARTH SCHOOL

I liken this earthly plane to a school for our souls—a place to learn, grow, and evolve. Life provides us with so many lessons, so look for them in all your experiences and interactions. One of the mottos I have in my life is: "It ain't over 'til it's over." Until our hearts stop beating, we are here for a reason. Once we have learned the lessons we came here to learn, we graduate and go back home.

It's difficult for us when our loved ones go home, especially when a child returns home, like Brian did. When this happens, many think they are leaving "too soon," but I believe that nobody leaves before their purpose is complete. It can be hard to understand how our Creator, a loving and all-powerful being, could let children die, but my rebuttal to this is, "Are you a loving parent when you send your child off to school and something bad happens to them, or when you take them to the playground, and they get hurt?" Yes, you are a loving parent, and so is our Creator.

The unpleasant and difficult things that happen to us in this lifetime are only temporary, because we never really die—we are eternal beings of energy, and in the big picture, nothing can truly harm us. The children who leave us to return home, are the brave souls who came to help us learn the lessons that accompany loss—they are our teachers. I feel that Brian was supposed to leave when he did, and that part of his purpose was to teach us about loss. Because of his bravery, we have learned valuable lessons that we couldn't have learned any other way, and we have grown so much.

Others stay for quite a while—yet we each take our turn, not knowing how soon or how long it will take for graduation day to come. The other side is our real home, and our trip to Earth is like going away to a special boarding school, so we can learn things that just aren't possible to learn at home. We are the ones who are away from home, and when we lose someone, they've simply returned home—a place where we'll all eventually be. What brings me comfort is remembering that death isn't an anomaly—it's going to happen to all of us at some point, and anyone we lose just happened to leave before we did.

As life continues, more loved ones will leave us behind, and eventually we will leave loved ones behind too. None are truly lost, as we will all be together again in the end. Our belongings will be forgotten and left behind, but what we bring with us are the relationships we've built and the memories we've made.

CHANGE

Throughout life, we are constantly experiencing change, and every change we encounter is a form of loss. My daughter loves acting, but endings are especially difficult for her—she gets very sad when any of her plays come to an end. One evening when she was having a hard time, I told her how life is a river of change, and it's about letting go of different things—over and over again.

I said, "You learned your lines, you sang your songs, and you danced your dances. You got to perform, and then it was over. Then, you went on to the next play, and you enjoyed all the things that it offered—until that ended. Be open to what's ahead, and what the next experience will bring—new lines, new songs, and new dances. But eventually, you will have to let go of those things, too."

The very first play that she was in changed her life—she had never acted before, and she landed a part with several lines. It sparked something special inside of her, and it was amazing to watch her come alive. When that play ended, she was grieving—hard. I wrapped my arms around her as she released her grief. She sobbed and sobbed as I sat with her and held space for her to move through her emotions After she let it all out, I could feel her sadness lifting. By cleansing herself of that heaviness, it enabled her to feel much better.

Grief visits us in so many ways besides death. Our lives are filled with grief every single day: the bittersweet process of watching our children grow, our own aging process, changes in our bodies, the end of a relationship, the closing of a favorite store, the end of a school year, the loss of a job, the loss of a home, or the loss of an heirloom. Although change is an inevitable part of life, if we can learn to flow with the changes as they come, then we can embrace life more fully and be able to adapt more easily to the inescapable loss of our loved ones.

RELEASING GRIEF | 193

QUANTUM LOVE

The famous quote by Alfred Lord Tennyson reads, "'Tis better to have loved and lost than never to have loved at all."

After my dad lost the love of his life, Teri, he would have done anything to have her back, and compares his grief to "an emotional kidney stone," yet he would do it all over again to have experienced the kind of love they shared. However, he countered, "She's been my booster shot to becoming a better me—but it's because she's *not* here." The growth that has occurred within him, he says, couldn't have come any other way.

The day he reunites with her can't come fast enough for him, but he says that her death and his grieving has pushed their relationship to another level—a *quantum* level, as my dad calls it. Each day he makes a commitment to her to become a better person, and talks to her spirit energy both morning and night. He has never missed a day in the vows he makes to her: to listen to others more than he speaks, to respond versus reacting, and to focus on helping others. His grief has brought him so many gifts, and I've witnessed my dad transform because of this sacred practice. I encouraged my dad to write down all the signs he's had, and continues to have, with his girlfriend Teri, and each experience is a treasure for him to reflect on.

FINDING SUPPORT

When we are grieving, we often feel alone. So, it's very important to seek support by reaching out to someone who will listen as you express your feelings, and who also possesses empathy for what's going on in your heart. Whether it's a friend or a therapist, talking to them regularly will do wonders.

We can also lean into community—connecting with neighbors, joining a gym, going to a bereavement group, attending church, taking a class, or participating in a book club. Being around others who can rally around you with love and support is priceless.

Mark your calendar with some things to look forward to—a vacation, going to lunch with a friend, participating in your favorite hobby, visiting a local spa, or going to a concert.

Get outside—being in nature and getting fresh air and sunshine can really help lift our spirits and move us into a higher vibration. Going for a walk is free, and moving your body helps to release emotions that may be stuck. Even something as simple as going barefoot on the grass can help ground you.

If you can find a way to laugh, it really is the best medicine. The very first time you laugh after you lose someone, it can feel wrong, but it is one of the best things you can do. One of the very first times I laughed after losing Brian was in the rehab one night as I watched a "Deep Thought" by Jack Handey, while watching *Saturday Night Live*.

Physical touch is especially important during grief. Get regular massages, hug the people you love, and give yourself a hug every night—especially if you live alone. You can do this by crossing your arms across your chest and giving your shoulders a tight squeeze. To make this even more powerful, imagine that you are getting a hug from your loved one as you do it.

Thinking outside of yourself by doing something for someone else can help, as well. When we focus on others by helping someone in need, or volunteering for a meaningful cause, we experience powerful healing. Journaling can also be therapeutic, as it allows you to express your feelings in a different way.

GAINING CLOSURE

Sometimes, there are situations in life where we don't get the closure we need. Generally, it's when something happens unexpectedly. Whether it's a sudden death, the unforeseen release from a job, or a relationship that ends without warning—it's a loss. If you can provide some closure for yourself—do it. Depending on the circumstance, there are many ways to do this:

1. Envision a scenario that has the ending you would have liked to have had.
2. Go say goodbye one last time. If you can't do this in person, then imagine doing it.
3. Say the things you never had the chance to say, whether it's out loud or in your mind.
4. Release balloons and imagine each one floating into a place of healing or into the arms of your loved one. You can write messages on them, or simply imagine the message you'd like to send.
5. Write a letter that you either keep or burn. The process of getting your feelings out through writing really helps release them.

Any of these practices can be very healing. Life is short, so give yourself the closure you need.

GETTING YOUR OWN SIGNS

Until you experience signs for yourself, it can be difficult to believe that it's truly possible. It's one thing to hear about someone else's experiences, but it's a game changer when you have your own personal experiences.

Remember that you and your loved one can develop your own unique way of communicating. Here are some of the ways that have worked for me in receiving signs from my loved ones:

1. **Be open** – Opening your heart opens the door to communication with your loved ones. We are all worthy of receiving signs—we just need to be open to the idea that it's possible.
2. **Be present** – Spirits vibrate at a higher frequency than we do, but we can raise our vibration by being present. Meditation, prayer, spending time in nature, and taking a break from screens, can help us become more present. Meditation doesn't require laying down or sitting in a certain pose; it can be done during daily tasks—it's simply

about being fully present in whatever you're doing. Creating through art, music, or writing, and leaning into emotions like love, joy, and gratitude, can help as well. I liken frequencies to a dial with three settings—high (spirit), medium (connection), and low (human). When we want to connect, our loved ones must lower their vibration, and we must raise ours. This allows us to "tune in" to the same frequency, where we meet in the middle—the medium—hence the term *spiritual medium*.

3. **Be aware** – Awareness is about paying attention. While some signs are obvious, others are subtle and require an awareness of the many things happening around you. Notice the recurring symbols in your life, the internal messages that surface in your mind, and the external signs you see or hear. The signs are there—we simply need to be aware of them. Along with this, moments when the energy in a room shifts, or thoughts of your loved one suddenly cross your mind, can be subtle signs that you've tuned in to their presence.

4. **Allow** – Although it's important to be aware, it's just as important to allow the signs to come in their own time and not seek them out like a treasure hunt. Just like the first time I asked Brian for an 82—it showed up as a miscalculation in my checkbook. I didn't realize I'd received my sign until I recalculated—because I wasn't looking for it.

5. **Connect** – Connecting with our loved ones draws them close. Spend time reflecting on your loved one—play their favorite song, look at their photo, watch videos of them, and reminisce about the good times you shared. Create a dedicated "landing spot" where you keep their photo and sentimental items—an area you can visit when you want to feel close. Connecting with them in this way

sends out a signal of love, inviting the connection you crave.

6. **Talk to them** – Speaking to your loved one continues building your relationship. It doesn't matter whether you speak out loud or within your mind; what matters is how heartfelt your message is. Listen for any thoughts that come to you, or any sensations you may feel. Act as if they are right beside you—because they are.

7. **Ask** – Asking is the key—it sets the stage and puts you on the same page. Asking encourages a response, like sending a text. When you're specific, they'll know what to send, and you'll know what to look for. Reading isn't believing, so try it for yourself and remember to be patient.

8. **Trust** – Know that your sign will come, and when it does, don't doubt it. Just as you trust an online order will be delivered, expect the same with signs.

9. **Thank** – Always offer genuine thanks to your loved one after receiving a sign. They will feel the love, and this appreciation will encourage them to send more.

Each time you receive a sign, write it down. You'll be amazed at how many you start to collect. Write them down as soon as possible, and keep a special journal specifically for this purpose. Reading through them will help you relive each sign and will aid in strengthening the connection with your loved one.

How do signs really work? Does it take skill for our loved ones to send a sign? Are there restrictions on the other side for how often signs can be given? I don't think anyone really knows for sure. Of the signs I've received, some I have asked for and others I have not. And of course, I haven't received a sign every time I've asked, nor from every loved one I've lost. We'll never truly know the parameters around sending signs, or why sometimes we don't seem to get them, until we take up residence on the other side ourselves.

I'm inclined to think that we interact with our loved ones during the night, as we sleep. However, it's extremely rare that we recall these interactions, as it could hinder what we came here to experience, and might increase our grief once we awaken. It's the same with the spiritual amnesia that we are all born with. If we remembered what it was like on the other side, it would defeat the purpose of life, and we would long to be there, instead of focusing on living our lives here. We are on this Earth and in these bodies for a reason—to expand and experience life in this realm, and to learn the lessons that can only be learned here.

It's easy to feel alone at times, but when you do, please know that there are *so* many souls on the other side who love you and are by your side, cheering you on throughout your life. Those souls consist of ones you've lost, and ones who you've known for eons— long before your journey here on Earth ever began. The other side is much closer than we think. Even though we can't see them, our loved ones are always there—just like the stars.

The near-death experiences that I've studied explain that death is a birthing process into another level of consciousness. They say it's as simple as closing your eyes in this world and opening them up in that world, and that there is *nothing* to fear. What awaits you is everyone, and every pet, you have ever known and loved, and it will be a grand welcoming full of absolute joy and tenderness. Experiencers also say that once you are there, it's clear that this life was the dream, and the other side is reality.

Each day, when you open your eyes, you have been given a gift to see another day here on Earth: another day to learn, to grow, and to love. What will you do with this day? Be intentional with your time, as once it passes, you can't get it back. Don't just simply exist; create meaning, and cherish the moments that you share with your loved ones, as each one ends as quickly as it came.

One of my favorite quotes, by Sir Francis Bacon, perfectly reflects this: "We have only this moment, sparkling like a star in our hand—and melting like a snowflake."

The accident was a tragedy, and I would do anything to have Brian back. At the same time, I know he is my angel now. I can see how much I've changed because of it—how, in many ways, it has been my greatest teacher. It has taught me to value what truly matters. I love harder, hug my kids tighter, and am grateful for both the storms and the bright days. I believe this life isn't the end—that we are eternal, and that love endures.

I'll leave you with the words written on Brian's headstone:

> In the end, we'll all be
> together again and
> find our way
> back home.

THANK YOU, READER

I appreciate you finding your way to my story and making it to this final page. I'm truly honored you took the time to read my words. Writing this book has been a difficult but healing process—helping me make sense of so much. I hope you felt my heart within its pages.

My wish is that this book has given you the courage to connect with your loved ones and recognize that you've been receiving signs all along. Your loved ones are not lost—they are always beside you, and they want you to "Keep that face."

With gratitude,

—Karin

If you'd like to connect or learn more, please visit my website at authorkarinmclean.com.

ACKNOWLEDGMENTS

To my brother, Brian, in loving memory: It's now been 33 years without you here in the physical. I feel so grateful to have had you in this life for the nine years that I did. I am also beyond thankful that you've shown us that you are still here. I am happy that you gave me the "Hell yes, sister!" to write this book, and for guiding me throughout the process. I can't wait to see you again someday, hug you tightly, and tell you how much I have missed you, face-to-face. I love you more than words can say!

To my husband, Shane McLean: Thank you for supporting me in following the nudges to write this book, for believing in me, and for creating my author website. I appreciate you sharing the special sign you received from your friend, and for allowing me to share it. I'm so thankful for the family we have created and to do this life with you by my side. I love you!

To my dad, Anthony Bozich: Thank you for your support, encouragement, and feedback while I wrote this book. Your words, "Even if you don't publish your book, you have done enough just by writing it," have brought me a lot of comfort. I love you and am very lucky to have you as my dad! Thank you for always sharing your sacred experiences about Teri and Brian with me, and for being so willing to let me share them here.

To my mom, Irene Bozich: The love and support you have given me, and continue to give me, mean the world. Thank you for always being there for me, no matter what. I am so thankful for the experiences with Brian that you've shared with me over the years, especially the drop of water sign you received, which opened me up to receiving one as well. Thank you for affirming my memory of choosing you before I came to Earth. I love you and am forever grateful to have you as my mother, and my friend.

To my sister, Erika Youngblood: Thank you for being so willing to share your experiences with me for this book. You are such a brave and strong soul to have survived the trauma of being the driver, which would have crushed most people—but not you. Thank you for your example of strength and resilience and for always being there for me. I love you, sis!

To my sister, Kristin Larson: Thank you for being my cheerleader throughout this process—your support has meant so much. I also appreciate you sharing your experiences with me. I am thankful that we had each other in the rehab center—we have been through thick and thin together, and I love you. Thank you for always being there for me and for always giving me your honest feedback.

To my Uncle Orin: Thank you for staying beside me during one of my first nights in the hospital. Thank you also for recording Brian's funeral for Kristin and me to watch later. That was so thoughtful, and although it wasn't the same as being there, it helped fill some of the emptiness we experienced because of not being able to attend in person.

Sandra Champlain: Thank you so much for endorsing my book. It is such an honor, which I will forever be thrilled about. Your book and your podcasts have reinforced my beliefs about the afterlife, and I am so grateful for your support. Thank you for sharing your light and for all you do; you are truly appreciated by so many.

Brynn Ahlstrom: Thank you so much for your incredible insights and editing work. The guidance you gave me in identifying what I really needed to say in certain areas has greatly helped me improve my writing. Your feedback and support have been invaluable. This has been an amazing journey, and I appreciate you so much!

Francine Platt: I love the book cover you made, and I thank you for designing one that truly resonated with me and the message of this book—it was exactly what I was hoping for.

Robert Harrison at Seneca Author Services: Thank you for formatting the interior of my book. You have a keen eye, and you have been so helpful!

Brent Mabey: Thank you for saving my legs, and my life! I am so grateful for all you did to save me, including being the only one who could successfully intubate me. I appreciate you being open and willing to answer all the questions I've had for you since. I am forever indebted to you. You are my hero!

Mary Mabey: Thank you for all you did at the scene of the accident, and for being so supportive of your husband. I appreciate you, your family, and your friends. I am forever grateful for all you have done, and for the questions you have been so willing to answer.

Martha Farney: Thank you for offering comfort to my mom and Erika during the accident, and for being willing to talk with me and share your perspective.

Mary Lou Klippell: Thank you for coming to our aid at the scene, and for being by Brian's side. Thank you for the things you shared with me. My family and I are forever grateful.

Donna Walker: Thank you for being the sweet soul that you are and for sharing your experience of seeing the glow around Brian. Thank you also for sharing your amazing experiences with scent and messages from your beloved husband, Ralph.

Nicole Suwinski: Thank you for sharing the visitation dream that you received from Brian. It was so comforting for all of us to hear. I know it was hard to lose your best friend at such a young age. Brian was so lucky to have you in his life, and I'm happy he got to experience having a girlfriend—I'm glad it was you.

Wynn McMillin: Thank you for being such a great friend to Brian. I appreciate you being willing to share the premonition dream you had about the accident. I know that it was a difficult thing to experience, and for it to then happen. Bless you.

Leanne: I am so glad you shared your beautiful experience with your father on social media, and that you gave me permission to share it here. It was such a magical sign, and has truly touched my heart.

Lauren Brielle: Thank you for being a great example and friend to me at a time when I really needed it. You were my candle in the darkness.

Amber Wanlass: Thank you for sharing the amazing signs you got from Brandon on the day he passed. The turkey couldn't have been a more perfect sign, and the rainbow was the cherry on top.

Kalie Bozich: Thank you for sharing the experience you had with Grandad in the hospital, and recognizing that "Somewhere out There" was one of Brian's songs. I love that you were able to experience this beautiful sign.

Cobie Bozich: I appreciate you texting me at special times when you've heard Brian's songs over the years—thank you.

Kari Van Wagner: I am thankful for the experience we shared together with the 82—it was so magical. I appreciate you sharing your other experiences regarding your mom, as well.

Dorothée Cannon: I am thankful that you recognized the sign from your mom. Thank you for letting me share.

Camille: Thank you so much for being willing to share your experiences with me. I really admire the strength that it has taken to be where you are today.

Carolyn Lundberg: Thank you for being so willing to share your sacred and beautiful experiences with me. I know they will help bring comfort to many.

Jenny Frazier-Relyea: Thank you for your incredible support during this process, you are amazing! I am so very grateful to have you as my friend. I also appreciate you sharing the amazing experiences that you've had with your dad. It is so incredible that he let

you know he was with you every time you and your family traveled to his favorite camping spot.

Jackie: You have been such a cheerleader for me throughout my
journey of writing this book. I appreciate all of your support and
thank you so much for reading through my proof copy with me, it
was extremely helpful. I am so lucky to have such a thoughtful and
caring friend. Thank you!

Mike J: I appreciate you letting me share your unique experience of sensing your dad's presence through smell.

Jen Whittaker: Thank you for sharing your story about the
message from your grandma with the logs on the freeway. What an
incredible experience! I love you and am thankful for your friendship!

Leticia Torres: Thank you so much for sharing your experience
with our neighbor and friend Lisa, which opened the door for me
to share my experience with you. It is amazing knowing that she
came to see us both.

Renee Tribe: Thank you for offering to read the very first copy of
my manuscript. I appreciate the suggestions you shared, and the
fact that you offered means so much to me.

Emily Cheney, Cheney Coaching LLC: Thank you for being
such an amazing life coach, and for helping me figure out my
"why" for writing this book. It really helped get me going!

Sarah Banks: Thank you for being such a caring person, for
coming to the hospital when my son was admitted, and offering me
the support I needed, mother-to-mother. I will never forget the
kindness you offered me that day.

Jenna Milligan: Thank you so much for reaching out to me the
day that Troy passed. If you hadn't, I wouldn't have found out
when I did. I really appreciate your thoughtfulness in doing that.

Traci Rosvall: I am so grateful that you were one of the first
people I saw after the accident, and for the friendship that blos-
somed because of that. I love having you in my life!

Robert Anderson: You were such an instrumental part of my

healing after the accident. You brought so much life and laughter to me and Kristin in the rehab center—thank you.

Amberly Read: Your kindness and forgiveness after the incident with your sweet dog, Lucy, brought my heart so much healing—thank you. You have such an understanding and loving soul, and I am grateful for the insight I gained because of what happened.

Kreg Weight: Thank you for sharing your experience on social media with the little girl who acted as an earth angel for you. I appreciate you letting me share it.

Liz: I am so thankful for all the memories we have made together over the years. I love that one of them includes your mom and Brian showing us that spirits can work together to deliver signs. I know she is right beside you and is watching over you.

Gwen: Thank you so much for allowing me to share your experience with Betty and the Matriarchs. It fills me with joy that you asked her for a sign and that she came through for you and your friend.

Danielle Christiansen/Dani C Photography: Thank you for the wonderful headshots for my book, and for always capturing memorable pictures of my family and me over the years.

And a shout out to all my amazing friends, and everyone in my life, who have listened to me talk about my book and for cheering me on throughout this journey.

And of course, a heartfelt thank you to all the departed loved ones whom I have referenced throughout this book—I am so thankful to you all for sending these beautiful signs, which can inspire us with hope and bring us comfort.

With all my heart,
Karin XO

ABOUT THE AUTHOR

Karin McLean's spiritual awakening was shaped by tragedy and healing. After narrowly surviving a devastating car accident that claimed the life of her younger brother, her life was forever changed.

In the years that followed, Karin began receiving signs from him —subtle, powerful, and impossible to ignore. These profound experiences ignited a deep exploration into what lies beyond this life, leading her to study near-death experience (NDE) accounts and ultimately recognize her own NDE as part of her awakening.

Drawing from her own spiritual encounters, as well as those shared by family and friends, Karin writes with the heart of a believer, offering stories meant to comfort, inspire, and remind readers that those we love are never truly gone. Her work is rooted in the belief that even in our darkest moments, there are gifts waiting to be found.

She earned her Bachelor of Arts in Communications from West-minster University in 2004 and has nurtured a love for writing for as long as she can remember. When she's not writing, Karin enjoys spending time with family, connecting with friends, working out at the gym, capturing moments through photography, walking in nature, reading, listening to music, and attending concerts. With an open heart and curious spirit, she continues to discover new perspectives on the afterlife, spirituality, personal growth, and health.

www.ingramcontent.com/pod-product-compliance
Lightning Source LLC
Chambersburg PA
CBHW021623120626
46545CB00001B/372